Yours affectionately.
William Aitchison—

FIVE YEARS IN CHINA;

OR,

The Factory Boy made a Missionary.

THE

LIFE AND OBSERVATIONS

OF

Rev. WILLIAM AITCHISON,

LATE MISSIONARY TO CHINA.

BY

REV. CHARLES P. BUSH, A. M.

"I will bring the blind by a way that they knew not."—Isaiah xlii. 16.

PHILADELPHIA:
PRESBYTERIAN PUBLICATION COMMITTEE,
1334 CHESTNUT STREET.
NEW YORK: A. D. F. RANDOLPH, 770 BROADWAY.

STEREOTYPED BY WESTCOTT & THOMSON.
JAS. B. RODGERS, PR.

PREFACE.

THE following pages have a two-fold interest and purpose; first, as the record of a pure, devoted life, full of strange providences; and, secondly, as a book of careful and accurate observations in a far-off and peculiar land, of which we know so little. It will be seen that the blind was led by a way he knew not; and that the land of Sinim is one of wonderful proportions and of marvelous interest.

We are much indebted to Rev. J. S. Burdon, of the English Church Missionary Society, and to Miss L. A. Andrew, of New Haven, for assistance in getting together the materials for the work.

It is humbly hoped that the volume may do something to encourage young men struggling against obstacles to enter the ministry, and something to aid in diffusing a more general interest in the all important subject of missions.

C. P. B.

ROCHESTER, N. Y., *November*, 1864.

CONTENTS.

CHAPTER VI.

CHAPTER VII.

CHAPTER VIII.

CHAPTER IX.

CHAPTER X.

CHAPTER XI.

CHAPTER XII.

CHAPTER XIII.

CHAPTER XIV.

CHAPTER XV.

CHAPTER XVI.

CHAPTER XVII.

CHAPTER XVIII.

CHAPTER XIX.

CHAPTER XX.

FIVE YEARS IN CHINA.

CHAPTER I.

Embarkation—Early History—Conversion—Aspirations—Education.

Ho for China! the land of hoary superstitions and ancient idolatry.

The good ship Candace is weighing anchor. The steam tug takes her in tow, and away they scud down the narrows, and out upon the broad ocean. There are two young men on board, just starting for the long voyage. One of them, through whose eyes, more particularly, we propose to look at that far-off country of the misnamed "Celestials," has already led a chequered life; so peculiar indeed as to suggest our motto, and justify a more particular introduction to our readers, before we proceed further with the long journey which he has undertaken.

His name is WILLIAM AITCHISON. He was born of humble parentage at Glasgow, Scotland, on the 4th of January, 1826. His parents came to this country in 1834, and soon after settled in Greeneville, Conn. Here the boy William was sent for a short time to the public-school, where his attainments were highly creditable, although not at all of the order of youthful prodigies. But even as a boy, his deportment was characterized by so much of sobriety and thoughtfulness, by such a spirit of inquiry and thirst for knowledge, that he always seemed older than his years.

At the age of twelve, however, he was taken from school, the place which he greatly loved, and set to work in a cotton mill for which he had no special affection; but nevertheless, in this humble occupation, he spent about two years, always faithful to his employers, although he was still eager after knowledge, scrupulously devoting every leisure moment to reading and study. Many an instructive volume did he devour, even whilst busy with his work, laying his book upon the machine to which he was attending, and catching a few sentences as he passed and repassed, with

Getting an Education.

Five Years in China. P. 10.

plenty of leisure in the intervals to digest all thoroughly, or store it away, in some quiet chamber of the memory, for future use.

He had, in the mean time, become a diligent and attentive scholar in the Sabbath-school, a constant and earnest listener in the sanctuary. His marked attention, indeed, to the preaching on the Sabbath, had attracted the notice of the pastor, and of others, while he was yet a stranger: and they had inquired him out, sent for him, and finding how desirous he was to improve himself, had loaned him books, and spoken to him words of counsel and cheer. When asked afterwards, why he listened with such fixed attention to the preaching, if it was because he was serious, or troubled about himself, he said, no, he was listening to gain knowledge.

But the day of his merciful visitation was at hand. There was no revival, no general seriousness, and no striking providence, in mercy or in judgment, to arouse his attention. God chose him in another way. As he was poring one day over an interesting volume in the mill, some of his young companions wished him to come out and join them in their sports, but he preferred to remain with his book. They urged their entreaties with clamor and vehemence, until at length he became thoroughly irritated, and let fall, it is believed, the first and the last profane oath which ever escaped his lips. He was startled at his own words; he was alarmed for himself; he did not before know that his heart contained such wickedness; and this was the beginning of his conviction of sin. He then for the first time felt that he needed a Saviour; and he sought and found Jesus Christ, the Lamb of God, that taketh away the sin of the world.

"He examined," said his pastor, "every step which he took, expressed nothing which he did not feel and believe, and when he came to the point where he submitted his heart to God, his act was intelligent, and from that time his course was onward; he was ready to perform any duty which was made known to him, and he began at once to labor and pray for the conversion of others."

When afterward a student in the Theological Seminary, he wrote in respect to this period of his life:—"You cannot imagine with what interest my thoughts cling around some spots in Greeneville. Not the least interesting locality is the room in the mill where, I trust, the Holy Spirit first arrested my attention, and directed my thoughts to the interests of my soul. Many a happy day did I spend in that room. While my hands were busy with my work, my soul was communing with God. I can go also to more than one rock or tree in the woods, at whose base, in the dark night and in the broad day, in the dreary winter and in mild summer, I often knelt to pray." And it is related also that with one young friend, whose hopes like his own had gone heavenward, he used to hold a daily prayer-meeting, long before the Fulton Street meeting was established. After taking their hurried mid-day meal, these two would go away alone to their holy trysting place in a neighboring grove, and there spend a portion of their brief respite from toil (only three quarters of an hour) in prayer to God, for mercy, guidance, usefulness.

His conversion occurred in the spring of 1840, when he was fourteen years of age. He continued to work however for a year or two longer in the cotton-mill, but not very contentedly; his thoughts and hopes were constantly soaring above and beyond that narrow sphere of labor. Indeed, almost from the hour of his conversion his mind turned to the holy ministry, and in a special manner also, *to the work of missions.* And now, more than ever, he desired on education; but how to get it did not yet appear. First, however, having indulged hope in Christ for nearly a year, he felt called upon to make a public profession of his faith.

His examination was highly satisfactory, and he was cordially welcomed to the fellowship of the Congregational Church in Greeneville, in the first Sabbath of March, 1841; he then being fifteen years of age. This step, manifestly undertaken with careful self-examination and prayer, served not only to deepen the work of grace in his own soul, but also to call out renewed expressions of interest in his behalf, and promises of aid, if he would undertake to prepare himself for the work of the ministry. Thus encouraged, he gladly turned his back upon the cotton mill, and again entered school.

His entire preparatory course was passed in the public-schools of Greeneville; they being at that time among the very best in the state, as they were the first to adopt the graded system and all the modern improvements; and Mr. Aitchison was not the only man of mark who went out from them. Here he pressed on rapidly with his studies; while the manifest purity of his character and nobleness of his purpose were adding constantly to the number of his friends and helpers, although he was never taken up and carried along without his own exertions. From all sources he received only enough of aid to keep him from giving up again and again in utter despair. From the beginning he endured hardness as a good soldier, proving that it is no disadvantage really to struggle with and surmount obstacles.

While yet a boy Mr. Aitchison began a religious Journal, from which we give a few extracts, to show the working of his mind at that early day.

"Aug. 9, 1842. Awoke this morning feeling my heart drawn out in love to God, and with a determination to serve him with all my strength through the day. I feel that my studies are a drawback to my growth in grace, and am sometimes almost ready to give them up; but then I think of Payson, who estimated the progress he made in his studies by the progress he made in holiness.

"Jan. 4, 1843. This is my birth-day; one among the many landmarks of my journey. Many are the interesting reflections which crowd into remembrance. God has ever dealt mercifully with me. While in my carnal state, (if indeed I am not so now), he preserved me from many dangers, and, as I humbly trust, led me by his Holy Spirit to the Rock that is higher than I. I desire to be wholly devoted to Jesus, and now consecrate to him my time, my talents, my life, my all.

"Jan. 18. Never did I realize the responsibility of my situation as a Sabbath-School Teacher. It is now about a year since I began this work; but in looking back upon my course, I can see that I have been entirely unfaithful to the souls committed to me. I have never realized, to any good degree, their worth, nor the solemn fact that I must meet each one of my class in the day of Judgment, and give account of the Sabbaths we have spent together. O that I may hereafter be faithful to them; that it may be the great aim of my labors and prayers to bring them to accept the salvation offered by the Saviour.

"March 12, Sabbath. I have thought much within the last few months, and especially since the meeting of the American Board in this place, of the millions who are perishing without a knowledge of the Redeemer, and of the duty of Christians to do all that lies in their power for the missionary cause. God is manifesting his willingness to do a great work in the earth, if Christians will but awake and do their duty.

"April 17. How thankful I should be to God for all his abundant mercies to me. But a few days ago my path was dark before me. I expected to be compelled to relinquish my studies, for a season at least; but now I have the prospect of continuing them this summer; and then I trust God will open the way still further.

"When all thy mercies, O my God,
My rising soul surveys,
Transported with the view, I'm lost
In wonder, love and praise."

And now, in view of this, how should I live? Certainly not cold and indifferent, as I often am, but full of love to the Saviour, and zeal in his cause. I think I feel to day more than ever that Christians should go about doing good. Lord may I have a heart to feel for the souls of others; and may I do good day by day.

"May 25. Have been engaged reading the memoir of Harriet Winslow. Oh, that I had her zeal, her love for immortal souls, her ardent desire to do good. I think if I know my own heart, I do not wish to live unless I can aid in advancing the kingdom of the dear Redeemer, and can thus glorify my God. But I am looking forward to doing good, and am neglecting the opportunities which daily present themselves. May I endeavor every day to benefit the souls of my companions.

"May 26. Have felt to-day more and more that it is the duty of Christians to spend all their talents and time in endeavoring to glorify the Saviour. Have enjoyed some sweet seasons of prayer to-day, but am compelled to mourn my want of faith.

"Read this morning a missionary paper, entitled 'A call to personal labor as a Foreign Missionary.' I think if the way is plain before me, and if I am enabled to qualify myself, I shall be willing to preach the gospel in a heathen country, or anywhere else.

"June 4, Sabbath. I feel very anxious for the conversion of my Sabbath-School scholars, knowing that their souls are in a measure committed to my care, and that a fearful responsibility rests upon me.

"I am reminded of the heathen this morning, upon whom no pleasant Sabbath dawns, to whom no crucified Saviour will be preached. O Lord, wilt thou raise up and qualify many who shall be willing to go forth and preach the gospel, even to the ends of the earth.

"July 15. I have this evening enjoyed a delightful season of prayer, and have consecrated myself anew to the Saviour. I feel that it is a precious privilege to give myself and all that I have to Jesus.

"I very much desire the conversion of my dear parents and sisters, who are now living distant from me. O Lord, visit them in mercy, and lead them to thyself.

"Aug. 6. Handed a letter on the subject of religion to G. B. W. to-day, praying that God would bless it to the salvation of his soul. O that I may realize the worth of the soul more and more each day.

"Aug. 8. Went to-day with two of my companions down the river four or five miles, distributing tracts among the Irish families upon the rail-road. Most of them are Roman Catholics, yet in nearly every instance they received the tracts apparently with great pleasure.

"Aug. 13. Sabbath morning. Since I became a professor of religion, I have always felt it to be my duty to preach the gospel of Christ, and to preach it to the dying heathen. After at least six or seven months of examining the subject and praying for divine guidance, I resolved this morning in the presence of God, to devote my life to the work of preaching the gospel to a heathen nation, if He in his good providence shall open the way. I have not come to this resolution without much consideration. I have read many books upon the subject; and, as I hear the cry of five hundred millions of souls who are perishing; as I hear the earnest appeals made by them through the missionary; and as I reflect upon the small number who dedicate themselves to this work, I am constrained to feel that I ought to offer myself, though poor and unworthy."

In 1844 Mr. Aitchison entered the Freshman class in Yale College. What his course was as a student there, will appear from the following testimony of Rev. Mr. Blodget, who was his classmate during seven years of study, and afterward his associate in Christian labors. "The first time I remember to have seen him, was in our class-meeting the first Sabbath morning after the commencement of the term. The exercises had been opened by a member of the senior class, who then gave place and retired from the room. After he had gone, Mr. Aitchison, then a young man of eighteen years, rose from his seat and with unaffected modesty and characteristic simplicity and fervor poured forth the language of his heart.

"Such was the beginning of his course in college, and such he held fast to the end. What he was in the first meeting, he was also in the last. During his entire college course he was always steadfast on the side of right and good order; and he became a pillar of the truth in the whole college community. Early in his course he was chosen a member of the church committee for that division of the class to which he belonged, and in that office, as well as in all his intercourse with his fellow-students, he won their respect, and in an unusual degree their love."

Nor was his influence confined to the college. Early in his Sophomore year he became a teacher in the Mission Sabbath-School, for colored people, in Broadway, and continued in the good work through the rest of his course of study. After serving three years as teacher, he was, upon graduation, elected Superintendent, and as such served three years more, spending much of his leisure time in visiting the sick and destitute among this poor people, by whom his labors are still kindly and gratefully remembered.

During a part of his college life, he was also one of the editors of the Yale Literary Magazine, showing the estimate in which he was held by his fellow-students as a writer. His contributions to the Magazine, in prose and verse, were numerous and highly esteemed. At three different times also he bore off the prize for excellence in composition. And all this whilst struggling with great embarrassments, compelled to teach a part of the time, acting also as Librarian to the college, in order to hold on his way.

Mr. Aitchison graduated in 1848, with credit to himself, taking the second honor of his class, the salutatory. Two years afterward he was appointed a Tutor in Mathematics in his noble alma mater, thus receiving the highest testimonial of the officers of the institution, not only to his superior scholarship, but also to the worth and weight of his character.

We have dwelt the longer upon the earlier part of Mr. Aitchison's life, because it is the key to the whole, and is full of encouragement to all who are struggling with like difficulties, or fondly cherishing similar hopes; and there is the more to cheer and encourage in his example, from the very fact that he was no prodigy, thus showing that transcendent gifts and brilliant endowments are not necessary to great usefulness, or to the highest nobility of character. But it should also be observed that he was never a drone, and never a rebel against decent restraints. He did not supinely trust to luck to get him over hard places; neither did he think it necessary to sow his "wild oats," or play any foolish college pranks in order to demonstrate his wit, or make himself an agreeable companion of his fellow-students. He was cheerful and playful, but never "fast" or furious; thus proving that college vices are not necessary to college popularity, for he was a universal favorite.

Mr. Aitchison pursued his Theological studies in connection with the Divinity school, at New Haven; attending at the same time, during the third year in the Seminary, to his duties as Tutor in the College ; and here also he was always the diligent student, the humble Christian, and the exemplary man.

CHAPTER II.

His Marriage—Begins Preaching—In Kent—Woodstock—Fitchville.

In the spring of 1851 (April 22,) Mr. Aitchison was married to the object of his early and devoted attachment, Miss Mary E. Andrew, daughter of Rev. S. R. Andrew, long the well-known and highly esteemed Pastor of the 1st Congregational Church in Woodbury, Conn., but then a resident of New Haven. Miss Andrew was a person of superior intellect, culture, and loveliness. They were kindred spirits, and both anticipated greatly augmented usefulness as well as happiness by their union. Often had they communed together, most tenderly and sacredly, about the Master's service ; and both had thought especially of the blessed missionary work ; but the health of Miss Andrew had been so feeble, even for years before their marriage, as to forbid their entertaining seriously, at least at that time, the thought of going to the heathen.

Mr. Aitchison was licensed to preach by the New Haven East Association, on the 5th of August, 1850; but he was not released from College duties or Theological studies until the summer of 1851. And now the day for which he had been fondly, eagerly hoping and praying for more than ten years had at last come—*he was prepared to preach the gospel.* He had indeed been made a Tutor only the year before; and those who receive that appointment, are expected to discharge the duties for at least two years; but Mr. Aitchison had expressly stipulated that he might lay them down after one. He would not accept the post save on condition that he might retire and enter at once upon the ministry as soon as he had completed his Theological studies. He would not let anything keep him one hour longer than was absolutely necessary from this his chosen work; this, which he regarded as the most honorable and delightful of all human employments.

As soon therefore as he had fairly accomplished the entire course of study, with a heart full of joy and hope, he began to look about for a place where to preach the unsearchable riches of Christ, to dying men. But, contrary to his own expectations and those of his admiring friends, for more than a year no opportunity for settlement, such as he desired, or such as all thought he had a right to expect, presented itself. God had other work for him; God's plans were deeper than his. He was indeed constantly employed, preaching in several different places; and was formally invited by two or three of the churches, to settle as pastor; but believing in his inmost heart that neither of these was a call of God; or, that the places did not offer sufficient inducements as to permanence and usefulness in the settled pastorate, he declined all.

One of the churches to which he so preached, and where he was called to settle, was that of Kent, Connecticut. Here with his beloved wife, he passed three months, from Oct. 1851 to January 1852, with manifest acceptableness and usefulness. To show how he entered into these fearful responsibilities of the ministrial office, almost as a veteran at the very beginning, we give a few extracts from his Journal, kept at the time.

"Oct. 23. This evening we have had a room

full of callers, and the hours have glided pleasantly and swiftly away. Oh! that the time may soon come when the question on the lips of every visitor shall be, 'What must I do to be saved?' I feel more and more the weakness of man, and I trust more and more the power of God to reach and influence the hearts of sinners.

"Oct. 25. Was told that a young lady, Miss H., desired to s e me. She has been somewhat unwell for seve al days, and is generally in feeble health. Dr. H. accompanied me to her house; and after attending to his professional duties, he, with the rest of the family, withdrew, leaving me alone with Miss H. No sooner was the door closed than she burst into tears, exclaiming, 'Mr. Aitchison, I want to be a Christian.' As faithfully and tenderly as I was able, I set forth the fullness and freeness of the salvation offered in the gospel; and endeavored particularly to lead her to realize the infinite love of the Saviour, and his willingness to receive and bless *her*. She opened her mind to me with considerable freedom, and seemed just entering the door of life.

"Oh! what an encouragement is an incident of this nature to one just commencing the work of the ministry. My heart has been rising in prayer for her ever since, and I cannot but hope that she will soon find in Jesus that peace for which she is seeking. Blessed Saviour, gather her in Thy fold, and make her one of the lambs of Thy flock.

"Nov. 3. Made three calls, two of which were on sick persons. One of these is a lady who seems to be in the last stages of consumption; but the chamber of weakness, languishing and pain, is manifestly as the gate of heaven. The world seems to have lost all place in her thoughts, and *Christ is all in all.* She is almost to be envied.

"Nov. 4. Walked this morning in a snow-storm, and called on Miss H. Found her much better, both in mind and body. She indulges the hope that she has passed from death unto life, and seems to be very happy. Her burden and darkness were all gone. The change was experienced on Sunday, Oct. 26th, the day after I saw her. Oh, how refreshing is such an incident. The Spirit has not utterly forsaken us. May this be but a drop before a plentiful shower.

"Nov. 14. At the church meeting this afternoon I talked to the church members as plainly as I was able, in regard to their *backsliding* and their duties, and I trust it will not be in vain. Deacon F. made some excellent remarks; and, on the whole, the meeting was one of more than ordinary interest. At its close a good lady besought me, with tears in her eyes, not to be discouraged.

"Nov. 16. Preached twice to-day to attentive and apparently solemn audiences. Felt exhausted by the labors of the day. This evening read in the memoirs of Brainerd. What a heavenly spirit! What a death-bed experience! Oh that all may follow him, so far as he followed Christ. I cannot rest contented till God grants us an outpouring of the Spirit. Oh how useless will be the most pointed preaching without the influences of that renewing agent.

"Nov. 19. Went to Macedonia. Preached to a full, attentive and solemn audience in the schoolhouse. It seemed as though the Spirit was among the hearers. Felt the importance of following up the public preaching with private conversation. Oh! how much Christians might do in deepening the impressions received from the pulpit.

"Nov. 23, Sabbath. Preached twice to-day. The weather was favorable, and the audience of moderate size. The afternoon sermon was particularly well received. But oh! the fruits! the fruits! God grant that I may soon see the *fruits* of my preaching!

"I long to enter the sanctuary again as an auditor, that I may enjoy the preaching of the word. It is in some respects a glorious and happy thing to be the *preacher;* but then the crushing weight of responsibility deprives me of ease and serene pleasure.

"Jan. 1, 1852. Another year, with all its joys and sorrows, its cares and labors, its sins and short-comings, has gone to join its predecessors in the gulf of the mighty Past. God has displayed nothing but his goodness to me through all its days and months. He has blessed me with almost uninterrupted health, prosperity and happiness. On the other hand what indifference I have manifested toward him! How cold have been my affections, how earthly my aims, how meager my attainments in holiness! Let this new year, if I am spared to see its close, witness greater faithfulness in the cause of Christ; more earnest labors for the salvation of souls, more rapid advances in the divine life. O Lord, to thee I cheerfully commit myself, my dearest wife, and all our interests. Do thou guide us in the path of life, bless us with thy presence, sanctify us by thy Spirit, and prepare us equally for life or for death."

At this point Mr. Aitchison's Journal is abruptly broken off, and is not resumed for more than a year. Soon after the above record was made he left Kent; preached for a few Sabbaths in Woodstock, and other places; passed a part of the summer with his wife, at New Haven, where a daughter was given to them; but finally engaged, the fall of 1852, to preach for a year at Fitchville, a small manufacturing village seven miles from Norwich.

There was no church organization in this place; but Mr. Asa Fitch, the wealthy proprietor of a large cotton mill, having the sagacity and nobleness to appreciate the importance of religious influences in a community, had erected a very neat Gothic Chapel; made provision for the minister, and invited the people, of all denominations, and no denomination, to come in, and freely occupy the house, and hear the preaching of the gospel.

Mr. Aitchison seemed to be just the man for this place. His catholic spirit, his great simplicity, and his true benevolence enabled him to win all hearts. God came also with his special blessing, and gave an entire year of deep religious solemnity, with a goodly number of hopeful conversions, as the reward of the diligent and judicious labors of his servant. And in all this, it was known that the heart of the minister greatly rejoiced. For a time also he had other comforts. Mr. Fitch, not only paid the minister's salary, which was liberal compared with those of neighboring parishes, but provided also a beautiful house as a parsonage. This was embowered in trees, surrounded with fruits and flowers, shrubs and plants, of almost every variety, both native and exotic; and there were shaded walks, and cooling fountains, skirted by a crystal stream and meadow lawn, with singing birds in leafy bowers, and ripe clusters of Eshcol from pendant vines—everything indeed to make the place as much like a little Paradise as it well could be.

CHAPTER III.

His First Sorrow—Loneliness and Sadness—Revival—Spiritual Body—Remark of Chrysostom.

MR. AITCHISON, with his loving wife and an infant daughter, moved into this beautiful home in the fall of 1852. Both husband and wife were peculiarly fitted to enjoy all the sweets around them; both deeply interested in the works of nature and of art; both peculiarly fond of trees, birds, streams and flowers; and formed also as Mr. Aitchison was in an eminent degree, for domestic and social enjoyment, and at the same time with heart to work just as faithfully as possible for Christ, and Christ plainly blessing his work, his cup seemed entirely full. But, as if a voice from heaven had fallen in a clear sky, loud, distinct, stunning, it came, "*Arise and depart, for this is not your rest.*"

That lovely wife had entered into their new abode an invalid. She saw but little, even from the first, of the out-door beauties of their delightful home. She went but once into company, and that only to join a few friends at dinner, with their patron, across the way. Her feebleness soon gave unmistakable signs of pulmonary disease; and her decline was so rapid that in less than four months she had completely withered, like the autumn leaves around her, and her mortal remains were carried back to New Haven for burial. Then fruits and flowers had lost all their sweetness to the afflicted survivor; and that beautiful embowered home, into which he had entered but as yesterday, with so much of hope and joy, was more like a prison than a paradise. Husband never mourned for wife more sincerely, more deeply, than he. Let us listen to some of the wailings of his poor, broken heart. We can hardly imagine anything more sad and touching than a large portion of his journal about this time. His burden seems greater than he can bear; and yet, like Job, he keeps his integrity.

"Feb. 25, 1853. My darling Mary has now been in heaven a little more than six weeks,—to me weeks of loneliness and desolation. Every day deepens my sense of bereavement, and adds to the poignancy of my grief. And yet I am not without rich consolation in the assurance that God doeth all things well, and that my loss is her gain.* These two considerations are inexpressibly comforting, especially when connected with the hope of re-union in a short time. Oh! that my affections may be effectually weaned from earth, and made to centre in God. Oh! that this grievous affliction may result in my own sanctification, and in blessings to this people among whom I labor. There are even now some indications of good. The prayer-meeting last evening was fully attended, and three persons remained for personal conversation on religion. Lord increase the number of sincere inquirers.

"Feb. 27, Sabbath. This day has been full of interest to me, and will be remembered in eternity. My precious, motherless child was baptized into the name of the Father, and of the Son, and of the Holy Ghost. Her grandfather administered the ordinance. Oh! what sadness filled my heart, what sorrow almost overpowered me, as I stood *alone* before the altar. There my Mary expected to stand with me and join in the

* See Obituary in Appendix.

solemn service of consecration just three months ago. But our God and Father (his will be done,) had other plans and purposes in regard to us. *She* stood before the *throne in glory* during the performance of the rite, while I stood before the altar in the earthly temple. Was that sainted one a witness, and an *interested* witness of the ceremony? Will she still watch over the sweet daughter, who will have no remembrance of a mother? Does she even now sympathize with me in my feelings and responsibilities? Alas! the Bible returns no definite answer, and reason dare not affirm with confidence. Let me, however, derive consolation from the *possibility*, not to say *probability*, that she is our ministering angel.

"And now, O Lord God, accept this child which I commit to thee. Spare her life, if it may consist with thy righteous will. Renew and sanctify her heart, so that her earliest moral exercises may be pleasing to thee. Make her useful in the church and the world by employing her as thine own instrument in the salvation of many souls; and prepare her for thy presence above, so that our little family may be a whole family in heaven.

"March 2. The sun is shining brightly this morning, and now and then the note of the blue-bird is borne to my ear. All nature looks cheerful; and yet here I sit in sadness and in tears, because I see the sunshine, and hear the bird-music *alone*. She who welcomed the last spring with me, whose smile was gladness, and whose voice was melody, has left my side. For her, however, I cannot weep; for, this morning, she looks on fairer sights, and listens to sweeter notes than earth can furnish. God her Saviour is making her infinitely happier than I could. He is wiping all tears from her eyes, and leading her into green pastures and beside still waters.

"But for myself I mourn; for all my earthly hopes blasted; for all my plans frustrated; for all my joys annihilated. Well, let me look above and beyond the perishing objects of time and sense to the things that are unseen and eternal. Let my affections centre on Jesus Christ, the same yesterday, and to-day, and forever. Let me still rejoice in the Lord, and joy in the God of my salvation.

"Not the least of my consolations is the fact that God seems to be blessing my labors among this people. The attendance on the means of grace is increasing, and a solemnity seems to rest on the minds of the people. Christians are shaking off their slumbers, and sinners are beginning to inquire with apparent earnestness, what must we do to be saved? Last Thursday three ladies remained after the meeting was closed for personal conversation. And on Monday night, stormy as it was, seven came to my study for the same purpose. It will be a blessed result of my affliction if it should be the means of bringing sinners to God, and honor to Jesus.

"March 3. I find myself inquiring with an interest unknown before my beloved wife's death, into everything pertaining to the state of the pious soul in the unseen world. While led to see the scantiness of all definite information in regard to minor particulars of future existence, I am attaining a more distinct and satisfactory conviction of the truth of the great realities which are the subjects of divine revelation. I am inclining more and more to what may be called *materialistic* views of heavenly blessedness. *Body*, not flesh, or as Isaac Taylor styles it 'corporeity,' I am disposed to regard as the inseparable companion of the human spirit. I prefer to regard death, not as working a mighty change in all the conditions and modes of being, but as simply introducing the soul to another state, analogous to the present, and yet superior.

"These views, and the many conclusions to which they conduct, I am by no means prepared to pronounce certain, but they are assuredly the source of much pleasure in my meditations. Let me however be more anxious to cultivate a personal fitness for the saints' rest, than to speculate concerning its nature.

"March 10. A beautiful morning of cloudless skies and gentle winds succeeds yesterday's storm and gloom. Not so however in the world within. My feelings are not in harmony with the *cheerfulness* of nature; I trust they are in some measure with its *peace*. The very sunshine is oppressive to me, and the spring-like aspect almost unendurable. Last evening I felt, almost for the first time, inclined to cherish rebellious thoughts. Grace, I trust, enabled me to banish them; but I fear their return as the spring days come on. Can I, oh *can* I pass this long summer in separation from my Mary? *Perhaps* God in his goodness will not require it of me. Let me at least be constantly prepared for the summons which may come at any moment.

"March 12, Saturday, 10 P. M. A day of gloom without, and gloom within, is closing. A sadness which I cannot resist, and can hardly endure, has accompanied me, and still refuses alleviation. I have prayed for death, and it seems as though I could welcome it. But I must patiently abide God's time. Doubts and fears have troubled me exceedingly, coming between my sorrowing soul and God. I am hardly able to make the great doctrines of the gospel seem like realities. Oh for more faith! more light! Lord forsake me not utterly. Leave me not to dishonor or deny thee! In thee do I put my trust. To whom shall I go but unto thee, for thou alone hast the words of eternal life. Thou art the God of my salvation.

"March 13, Sabbath. Bless the Lord, O my soul, and all that is within me, bless his holy name. I feel this morning more cheerful than I have for a long time. Not that I mourn my darling Mary's absence any the less, but because I am able to raise my thoughts above the gloomy grave to the bright abodes of the saints; because God seems near and my Redeemer precious.

"Oh, how little need the Christian care what his earthly condition and circumstances are; Christ is his, heaven is his, and he ought to be satisfied. My precious wife may now be pitying me, and longing to welcome me to a participation in her superior joys.

"March 16. The Lord is comforting me with the sight of souls returning to himself; and permitting me to be an humble instrument in the dispensation of his mercy.

"April 22. The anniversary of my wedding. I fear that I am not sufficiently anxious to learn the design of God in bereaving me. If I am his child, it cannot be that he takes pleasure in my grief. What then does my Father intend? Of one thing I am sure; he would have me more entirely consecrated to the work to which I am called; more sensible of the comparative worthlessness of all created good. Oh that grace might enable me to rise above my sorrow, and use double diligence in the discharge of all my duties.

"May 23. My loneliness becomes constantly less endurable, and my heart, I fear, less submissive. There is an unceasing struggle within. I *know* God is good and merciful, but it seems difficult to *feel* it. I know the dreadful blow was given in love, but it is difficult to enjoy the consolation such knowledge is fitted to impart.

"A remark of Chrysostom which I met in reading Leighton's works, together with the Commentary of the pious Archbishop, struck me forcibly; 'Minatur ne cædat, cædit ne occidat'—'If speaking either mildly or sharply will prevail with his children, he will not stir the rod to them; and when the rod is in his hand, if showing or shaking it will serve the turn, he will not strike with it. But this is our folly; that usually we abuse all this goodness, and will not part with our sins till we smart for them, and be beaten from them.'

"Such seems to have been God's goodness in his treatment of me, and such my folly in my treatment of him. Had I returned from my wanderings when first my beloved wife became ill, she might possibly have been spared to me. My own obstinate sinfulness, it may be, rendered the infliction necessary. O, my God, help me to come to thee now, lest further chastisement be needful. Help me with renewed diligence to enter upon the performance of every duty, that I may enjoy thy smile.

"May 25. Have enjoyed more of the presence of God, and consequently, more peace to-day than for some time past. The Lord seems to be saying to the waves of doubt on which I have been tossing, 'Peace, be still!' Though feeling even more lonely than ever, so far as earth is concerned, my Friend above is unusually precious and gracious. Heaven appears, oh, how sweet and desirable. I long to enter it, but pray for patience to wait the Master's time.

"July 24. There are still many indications of God's presence among this people. The weekly-meetings are thronged with prayerful, zealous, active disciples, apparently willing to take up the cross and follow Christ."

CHAPTER IV.

Joys Remaining—Thinking of Missionary Life—His Child a Hinderance—Death of Child—God Making him a Missionary.

So ran the private record of his inner life. That it is entirely truthful we do not doubt; and yet we fear it would convey a wrong impression to many minds if taken by itself alone. It was the happy privilege of the writer to know him more intimately at this than at any other time; to welcome him often at the parsonage; to talk with him, in all the intimacy of a warm personal friendship, morning, noon and night; to go with him on various little excursions, with many a delightful drive over the beautiful hills of New London county; and in all these circumstances his mind yielded pleasantly and healthfully to the recreation. It was easy to see, indeed, that he was a stricken man and a sincere mourner. He loved to talk of his sorrow; and unbidden tears would freely flow, as he spoke of his beloved

Mary and his desolate home. But as we turned to Scripture themes, or to man and his institutions, his mind would kindle with its wonted enthusiasm, and there seemed nothing gloomy or morbid in his views. Indeed, he was often joyous and playful, laughing and romping with the children, as though he had always lived in sunshine. "Happy days," he afterward wrote from the far-off land of Sinim, "were those spent in your society, even though they were days of affliction." And again, "I often think of the golden hours we spent together. I recall with mournful pleasure the various scenes in which we were associated. Oh for another ride after old Billy! Oh for another talk in the snug parlor! Oh for another prayer and hymn together! Alas, it may not be!"

With real zest also he attended the monthly "ministers' meeting" of New London County, and with delightful interest and appreciation he entered into all the discussions, speaking on almost every question, and always speaking to the purpose. One occasion was especially memorable. The meeting was in New London; the subject for discussion being the *a priori* argument of Rev. Dr. Samuel Clarke for the existence of a God. Mr. Aitchison was chairman of the meeting, and it devolved upon him, after all the rest had spoken, to make the closing remarks. He rose and began with the simplest axiom, "From nothing, nothing is. But here is something, the world of matter and of mind. It must have had a cause—or be causeless, and therefore eternal. It is not eternal, for it is mutable. It must therefore have had a cause; and a cause adequate to such stupendous results must be God."

Thus discarding the abstruse and subtle theory of Dr. Clarke, as too etherial to rest upon, and taking the simplest proofs of divine existence as manifest in the works of creation, he gave, in a speech of about ten minutes, as all conceded, one of the most compact, terse, logical arguments upon that subject to which it had been the good fortune of any of us to listen. The sentences were truly Baconian as they fell from his lips; the argument symmetrical and complete. Not an unnecessary word was used; not a word could well have been spared; and all was uttered with just the same modest simplicity with which he would have spoken to a small Sabbath-school class, or to a friend in a private conversation. All present were charmed with the speech; and on many subsequent occasions it was referred to as something more than ordinary. Indeed, one of the foremost men of that meeting writing about it nine years afterward, while unable to recall the particulars, says, "The general impression on my mind, of remarkable discrimination and nice analysis, evincing rare mental discipline, I can never lose. Indeed, it is one of those passages in the history of a meeting, which has never wanted for passages, which stands out in bold relief."

Another interesting occasion is well remembered; a ride to Westerly, about twenty miles; the digging of rhododendrons, from a spot near Lantern Hill, on our return; the carrying home, in our small wagon, of four large thrifty shrubs, which his hands helped to set in front of the parsonage, where they still stand, in health and vigor, annually putting forth their wealth of bloom, a monument of one, at least, of his happy days. How he broke an old man's spade in the operation; and how we laughed at his attempt to extort from us eight times what it was worth to get it mended; and how we finally settled on more reasonable terms and parted amicably, need not be more particularly mentioned.

Another very little incident is vividly recalled. Sauntering one afternoon over the hill, on a back road, and in a lonely spot, "Stop a minute," he said, "and I will show you something." Turning a few steps to the stone wall by the way-side, reconnoitering a moment, he seemed to find the object of his search, and lifting a small stone which covered a hollow in a larger one, he came upon *four cents*, thoroughly blackened, as by long exposure. "There, said he, J—— and A—— and W——, (naming three of his particular friends, and former school-mates,) were walking this way with me eight years ago and we each deposited a cent in this hollow in the stone, to see how long they might remain here." And so saying, he covered them over again, and we went on our way. Curious conceit; curious Savings' Bank. The only purpose it seemed to serve was pleasantly to recall his friends, and to suggest many interesting things connected with them, upon which he enjoyed speaking as we went on our way.

And so even in these days of deepest darkness, some glimpses of sunshine came through the opening rifts. And yet that his sensitive nature suffered very keenly, and that when he sat down alone, or paced his desolate room, he was often overwhelmed, we do not doubt. That he did not actually question God's right to do as he would with his own; that he tried constantly to say "Thy will be done," is very plain. Nevertheless, the ways of Providence were, in his case, peculiar. In less than two years from their happy marriage, that fondly cherished wife, for whose sake, as he most conscientiously believed, he could not go far hence to the Gentiles, was torn from his loving embrace and laid cold in the silent tomb. With her dying breath she gently whispered, "Now William you can be a Missionary." But it was not she alone who said that; but a voice divine was heard, in every passing breeze, in every rustling leaf, and in the heavy thoughts of many a weary, wakeful midnight hour, saying the same thing. "My early missionary feelings and purposes"—he said—"all revived."

Thus *impressively* called to consider anew his

duty to the heathen, there still remained time for due reflection, and for consultation with friends, before absolutely deciding on such an important step, inasmuch as his engagement at Fitchville had six months yet to run. One very serious obstacle, moreover, lay across his path. That little daughter, his second Mary, now doubly dear to him because the first, whose sacred name she bore, was laid in the grave; for whose sake he often ran on to New Haven to pass a few days with the grandparents where she was staying, and to whom his attentions and caresses were devoted day by day, while he thought of the sainted mother; it seemed necessary that he should remain at home to take care of his child. "How," he asks, "could I bring virtual orphanage upon her? The struggle in my mind was severe and protracted." But we shall see how the Master enabled him to settle the question, and how the way for his feet was still more clearly marked out by the finger of Providence.

But first another quickening influence was brought to bear upon his mind. A devoted missionary from Africa passed a Sabbath by invitation at his house, and presented the wants of the heathen world to his people. To him he freely opened his heart, and from him he received words of counsel and encouragement. This led him to address a free and earnest letter to his father-in-law upon the same subject, from which we quote a few paragraphs.

"In view then of these particulars, and of the general claims of the heathen world; in view of Christ's last command and the fearful apathy of the church in respect to it; in view of my past exercises on this subject, and God's recent dealings with me, I am constrained to inquire seriously and prayerfully what my duty is. Do, my honored father, assist me in these circumstances with your counsels and your prayers.

"But you will inquire, Have you thought of the obstacles which must be surmounted, the crosses which must be borne? Yes; and these alone cause me to hesitate. How can I leave my darling child, tenfold dearer since her mother's death; and also my aged parents? Nature cannot endure even the *thought* of it; but the love of Christ may enable me cheerfully to bear the terrible reality. Did the path of duty seem clear, as it relates to these dear ones, to whom I owe so much, I now see nothing to hinder my going abroad. And yet I dare not say to God, although he knows all my thoughts, *that I will not go even now*, lest he take these dear friends out of the way by death.

"You see, dear father, my circumstances. Tell me, without reserve, your opinion. You may think it strange that I should for an instant harbor the thought of leaving my little one. Sometimes I think so too; but duty must be done, though every fibre of the heart bleed."

So he wrote on the fifteenth of August. A few weeks later, being in New Haven, he went over the matter more fully in a long conversation with his venerated father-in-law, and finally came to the distinct conclusion, that if he could set apart a portion of his small salary as a missionary to the support of his child, he would at once offer himself to the American Board, to go wherever they should direct.

So he left his friends in New Haven on a Saturday; so, with many passionate kisses, and not unmanly tears, he parted from his darling child, thinking how soon he was to leave her, almost cruelly, for the rest of life's journey; and so, with a heavy but peaceful heart, he returned to his parish duties for the Sabbath.

But swift-footed Mercury could not have outstripped the message which came the very next Monday throbbing over the telegraphic wires. "Your child is sick—you had better come on." This message came to the care of the writer, as the wires did not extend to Fitchville. Driving up as soon as possible from Norwich, he put the fatal document into the hands of the stricken man; and well does he remember how like a knell of death it evidently fell on his crushed heart. He read it all in a moment, even far beyond that one fearful line, and hastened as fast as possible to his dying child. He watched by his last fading flower about a week, saw every petal droop and fall, and then laid it away in the spot already consecrated by his precious dead. The question was now entirely settled; the child was perfectly provided for; and the fond father, once more heart-broken, and yet submissive and uncomplaining, turned to obey the Divine behest. Now he *must* be a missionary.

His next letter (Sep. 22) was in these words:

"The blow has descended, and I am childless!

No, I will not say that, for I still have a child—*in heaven.* My darling, after a very violent illness, with great suffering towards the last, died on Monday night. Yesterday we committed the lovely remains to the tomb, not without a *joyful* anticipation of the resurrection from the dead, and the life everlasting.

"This new affliction has stunned me. I seem hardly able to mourn. I am almost deprived of the power of thought. What is this world to me now? It is all disappointment, sorrow, suffering, darkness. There is, however, light *above.* I endeavor to raise my eyes to that, but my tears almost blind me even to its purity and brightness. Oh, pray for me, that I may not be left to murmur or despair! Pray that these almost overwhelming afflictions may result in my sanctification and more entire consecration. Pray that I may be willing to walk even in darkness, and yet trust in God."

In his Journal also he wrote, "Sept. 28. * * * * I write with a heart more sorrowful than ever before, more desolate, more hopeless. * * * * The only ray of sunshine which shone in my sky has been withdrawn; and now, so far as earth is concerned, *all is darkness.* I trust, however, that heaven is becoming more bright and more attractive. God by removing my treasures to his own abode, is drawing my thoughts thither also. Nothing now remains to occupy my attention and enlist my efforts but his kingdom and cause. Renewedly do I now consecrate myself and my all to him, praying that he will send me wherever he desires me to serve him, though it be to the ends of the earth.

"I set out this morning for Cincinnati, to attend the meeting of the Board. I intend to confer with the Secretaries in regard to my duty to become a missionary. The Lord guide me to a right decision."

A letter received from Mr. Aitchison immediately after his return from this meeting, (Oct., 20,) has these sentences, showing how impossible it was for him, even amid the shifting scenes of travel, to forget his griefs. "When we meet, I shall be happy to give you a particular narrative of all my adventures and experience since I saw you last. This much I will say, however; pleasure and happiness have been for the most part strangers to my bosom. Alas! change of place and of scene cannot mitigate our sorrow for the loved ones who have left us. Never has my grief been more pungent, my desolation more complete than during the present week. How sad, sad were my feelings as I traveled from New Haven to-day. One short year ago this very week, I came here a husband and a father; now I am a *widower* and *childless*. The meaning of those words I pray God *you* may never know. *Pray for me.*"

Still sad, therefore, and yet determined, and in obedience to the manifest will of the great Head of the church, Mr. Aitchison now wrote to the Secretaries of the Board at Boston, formally offering himself for the missionary work. After briefly mentioning the peculiar circumstances which had brought him to this decision, he says, "The path leading to heathendom lies before me clear as sunlight. I long to preach Christ among the Gentiles. Only in a pagan land can the cherished desire of my life have its fulfillment.

"As to my motives in thus seeking the missionary work, I trust I am actuated first by the love of Christ, and next by the love of souls. Other minor considerations, of course, have their weight with me; but these it is unnecessary to mention.

"As to my field of labor abroad, I at first thought of Western Asia, but circumstances with which some of the Secretaries are acquainted lead me now to prefer China. The numbers of the heathen in that vast empire, and the difficulties attending its evangelization render it additionally attractive.

"As to my health, it is excellent. I have hardly lost a month from sickness during twenty years. Though not apparently robust, my powers of endurance are, I think, more than ordinary."

The offer which he thus made of himself was readily accepted, and with equal alacrity he set about the needful preparation to go far hence to the Gentiles. Mr. Fitch and all that little flock to whom he ministered so acceptably and to whom he was tenderly attached, greatly desired him to remain with them. They used argument and entreaty; but all in vain. "I should not now *dare*," he said to the writer, "to remain in this country; I should not dare to make any arrangement, or lay any plan, which should prevent my being a missionary." "In obedience to

God's *reiterated* call," he said in another letter to the Secretaries of the Board, "I go to China."

It was still hard to part with surviving kindred and friends. "Keenly," he says, in a letter to his own parents, "shall I feel the sorrow of separation from all those I love; but still I rejoice in every self-denial to which duty calls. In this short life, what matters it *where* or *how* we spend the time, if only we are duly prepared for that *endless eternity*, upon whose scenes we shall soon enter?"

CHAPTER V.

His Ordination—Embarks for China—Storm and Peril—First Sabbath Service at Sea—Lines to New Haven—Efforts for the Sailors—Lines to a Certain Cottage in New Haven—Employment of Time.

MR. AITCHISON was ordained to the missionary work in the Second Congregational Church of Norwich, on the 4th day of January, 1854, which was his birthday, he then being twenty-eight years of age. The sermon was preached by Rev. Dr. Hawes, of Hartford; a solemn, appropriate, and peculiarly touching charge to the candidate was given by his beloved father-in-law; and it was the happy privilege of the writer, as a particular friend, to give him the right hand of fellowship, and in behalf of the Ordaining Council, to bid him a hearty God-speed in his glorious work. And it was but giving voice to the sincerest thoughts and wishes of all present, to assure him of their true respect, their entire confidence; and that their highest hopes and most earnest prayers should follow him even to the ends of the earth.

He was appointed, with the Rev. Henry Blodget, who was his college classmate, associate Tutor, and a fellow student in the Theological Seminary, to commence a mission at Shanghai. And these are the young men on board the good ship Candace, the 11th of April, 1854, bound for Canton. How they passed their time during the long voyage, what storms and calms, what sights and perils they passed, will appear, in part at least, from the following extracts from Mr. Aitchison's journal.

"At precisely half-past twelve we left the wharf in tow of a steam-tug. Last adieus were waved by and to the few acquaintances who stood upon the shore; and then we addressed ourselves to the task of keeping calm, while we penned a few farewell lines to the friends nearest and dearest. At about three o'clock the sails were set, the hawser which connected the bark with the tug cast loose, and we stood away China-ward, with a favoring breeze. Soon after sunset the heights of Never-sink were rapidly belying their name, by their disappearance beneath the waves.

"Before ten o'clock I retired to my berth for the night, after committing to God in silent prayer all my dear friends whose society has been so sweet, myself, and the great work to which I have devoted everything I have and am—the *Salvation of China.*

"April 22, Sat. Eleven days have passed since my last entry. During this long period, we have scarcely seen the sun. We have been traversing what are called in the charts the stormy regions of the Gulf Stream. Clouds, rain, wind, waves, sea-sickness, danger and misery—are the words which apply to the voyage thus far. The wind has boxed the compass more than once, blowing a gale from every point in succession. The morning after leaving New York there was for a few hours almost a dead calm. As we were on soundings, Mr. B. and myself got out our fishing gear, and went industriously to work. I had the honor of hauling in the only fish captured—a noble cod, weighing forty-two pounds. The next day the sky became overcast, the wind rose, the sea ran hill high, and our troubles commenced. Sunday morning at 1 o'clock, A. M., the violence of the storm compelled us to heave to. For

Five Years in China. The sea ran hill high. Page 62.

hours I contemplated death as an impending event, and looked into my prospects for eternity. Though deeply sensible of my sins, and desirous of living to do something for the redemption of the heathen nations, I think I was enabled to cast myself into the arms of my Saviour, and say, 'I am ready to be offered, if such is thy holy will.' God in his great mercy, however, protected us through all dangers seen and unseen; and to-day the ocean is comparatively calm, and the aspect of the heavens favorable.

"April 23, Sab. This day may be called, in a certain sense, my first Sabbath at sea, as I was only lasting, and not living, one week ago. Immediately after washing and dressing I went forward on the bow-sprit and enjoyed a pleasant hour of communion with God, and of meditation on holy themes. I read my Bible, sang and prayed aloud, my voice mingling with the murmur of the waves as they dashed beneath. Every thing seemed hallowed by the presence of God. There was, as I have often felt on shore, a seeming spell laid upon every object in nature, in token of the sacredness of the day. The sky was almost cloudless, the sun shining in his strength, the sea rolling majestically and yet gently, the air balmy but invigorating.

"After breakfast I consulted the captain in regard to the distribution of books and tracts among the crew; he gave his full and cordial consent to any efforts we might choose to make for the spiritual welfare of the ship's company; informing me at the same time, that it was his intention to call the sailors together and distribute among them books and tracts which the Bible and Tract Societies had furnished for that purpose. This was accordingly done, each man being furnished with a Testament and several tracts, in the language with which he was most familiar. It was interesting to see the eagerness with which all accepted the volumes, and more interesting an hour afterward to see them here and there on the deck in the shade, attentively reading what had been thus furnished.

"At eleven o'clock we held our first public religious service, which was conducted throughout by Mr. B. His discourse was very appropriate and practical, founded on Matt. viii. 1—4. The majority of the sailors,—I regret that I cannot say all,—were present, and listened with gratifying attention to all the exercises. Since dinner my time has been spent in reading Alleine's 'Heaven Opened;' and in conversing on personal religion with one of the mates. He labors under the mistaken notion that an officer of a ship cannot really be a good man; that he must swear now and then, or lose his authority over the men. He moreover tried to be a Universalist, for the sake of quieting his conscience, while living in the conscious neglect of every duty which he owes to God. I tried faithfully but kindly to show him his error and danger. While uneasy afterward from the fear of having offended him, he came up from below with a pair of new worked slippers in his hand, which he begged me to accept; testifying plainly by this act that he was not indifferent to my interest in his true welfare.

"On the whole, this day has been a Sabbath of rest to my soul. God has seemed near, Christ precious, heaven attractive. I have thought much of the past and the future; much of my loved ones living, and more of the dead. Quiet tears have stolen down my cheeks, which were not all expressive of sorrow. My heart is often full to overflowing. Visions of a blessedness which is unalloyed, and knows no end, are ever rising to my spiritual eye. Thought, and desire, and feeling are ever busy with what has been, or what is to be. Oh, that I could find my rest and my enjoyment more fully, more exclusively, in God. Then would every event be to me a blessing."

A few days later, Mr. Aitchison was taken quite unwell, and suffered considerably for a time. Then, more than ever, his mind turned back to scenes of other days; and "while suffering the most, and feeling the saddest," he says, "my thoughts, almost of their own accord, took the following form:

There is a hallowed spot,
Beyond the Atlantic wave,
To which my heart in sadness turns—
My much loved Mary's grave.

Within the church-yard gate
That hallowed spot is found;
Where stands a snow-white tablet,
There droops a grassy mound.

Beneath that grassy mound
Are wife and child asleep;
While I, a weary mourner,
Am left alone to weep.

But soon these tears will cease,
My wanderings all be o'er,
And husband, wife, and child, in heaven
Shall meet to part no more.

"April 29. Have had some cheering views of the future. Find myself frequently repeating, with prospective reference to my work in China, those lines which seem to have been favorites of the great Judson:

"In these deserts let me labor,
On these mountains let me tell
How he died, the blessed Saviour,
To redeem a world from hell."

"Oh, if I could but win some poor Chinese to Christ, how more than repaid should I be for all the self-denial it costs to go to that distant land! But let me remember that mine is the work; the result is of God. My life will not be in vain, I am confident, even though I should die before reaching my destination. My consecration, imperfect as it is, will, I trust, have some influence with others in leading them to the consideration of personal duty to the heathen.

"April 30, Sabbath. Early in the morning had a delightful conversation with Mr. B. on the nature of heaven's felicity. We are both of the opinion that much of the Scripture language is figurative; but I am more materialistic in my anticipations than he; more prone to speculate on the subject; perhaps less disposed to rest satisfied with the plain revelation of God in regard to all the future. I trust my conjectures, analogies, reasonings, and I may add, my hopes will never be at variance with divine truth. I long to know more about the condition of the departed. I love to think of the joys of the ransomed. I find profit in meditating on the glory that is to be revealed in the saints. Surely we can hardly think too much of heaven.

"May 1. Our arrangements for public religious exercises on board are mainly completed, and are as follows:

"1. A blessing asked before every meal by Mr. B. and myself alternately.

"2. Prayer every evening on deck, accompanied by the reading of the Scriptures, and the repetition of a hymn; conducted by us successively on alternate weeks.

"3. A sermon on the Sabbath, by us alternately, with the usual accompaniments of the Sanctuary.

"4. A Bible-class, on Sabbath afternoon, Mr. B. having one watch, and I the other.

"In general, Mr. B. is to have particular spiritual care over one watch, and I over the other. Oh! that the Lord may bless these efforts to the salvation of some among the officers and crew. We may surely take encouragement from what missionaries have sometimes accomplished in their voyages to and from their fields of labor. How glorious the results of Dr. Judson's prayers and efforts, on board the Ramsay, on that otherwise sad voyage from Calcutta to Maulmain, *via* Mauritius. Already the sailors manifest a deep interest in everything attempted for their soul's good.

"May 3. For the first time since the voyage commenced, I took down the Chinese books this morning, and began the study of the language in earnest. It looks truly formidable; but I can do all things through Christ which strengtheneth me. My forenoons will be mainly occupied in this way.

"May 8. My lonely musings have recently taken the shape of—

LINES

Addressed to a certain little cottage in New Haven.

Dear home of years! thy sacred joys
  Can never more be mine;
I ne'er shall see the friends I loved
  In days of 'Auld Lang Syne.'

And yet thy walls before me rise,
  Wrapt in the leafy shade,
Where, through the livelong summer's day
  The birds sweet concord made.

In dreams I visit thee again;
  Within thy doors I stand;
Familiar forms around me throng,
  And press my willing hand.

Once more my Mary's smile I see;
  Her low sweet voice I hear,
The one was music to my soul,
  The other to my ear.

Once more she tunes the light guitar,
  And sweeps the sounding strings;
While loving list'ners laugh or sigh,
  Moved by the songs she sings.

Time flies—to crown our wedded love,
  There came an angel child,
Whose face was like her mother's face,
  So fair, so glad, so mild.

Bright days of sunshine come and go,
  The future greets our eyes;
Within its realm, dim though it be,
  A home of beauty lies.

Together there we pray and toil,
  For sinning, dying men;
Together calmly sleep in death;
  Then live and love again.

The dream—dispelling morning breaks
  Along the path I tread;
And memory whispers to my heart,
  Thy joys and hopes are dead.

Dear home of years! farewell! farewell;
  Between us oceans roar;
May all who loved beneath thy roof,
  Soon meet to part no more.

"May 13. My eyes have turned eastward for the last few days towards the Gaboon Mission, West Africa. I almost envy the brethren there their retirement from all the turmoil of this world. I was strongly inclined at first to select that for my field. It has attractions for me which China does not possess. But my Master pointed to the land of Sinim, and I cheerfully go thither. But, dear fellow laborers, I heartily bid you God speed. Be not discouraged. The day is dawning on the nations. Even Ethiopia will soon be, if indeed she be not now, stretching forth her hands unto God. In the last day may you have the privilege of placing many jewels in the Redeemer's crown, whose reflected rays will brighten those that encircle your own brow."

The ensuing record indicates an earnest desire to make the most of his time.

"The following plan for spending each day I adopted some time since, and have seen no reason to make any essential change—six to eight o'clock, devotional reading and exercises; eight to eight and a half, breakfast; eight and a half to nine, recreation and miscellanies; nine to twelve, *study of Chinese;* twelve to one, recreation and miscellanies; one to one and a half, dinner; one and a half to four, general reading; four to five, writing in journal, &c.; five to six, devotional reading and exercises; six to six and a half, tea; six and a half to eleven, recreation, conversation, star-gazing, *thinking.*"

This last word is heavily underscored in the manuscript; and we know from his letters of what, in those lonely night hours, far out on the broad ocean, he was often thinking; of home, kindred, and loved ones, in this, and in the better land. "Never," he wrote about the same time to his parents and sisters, of whom he had taken sorrowful leave for all the rest of earth's pilgrimage, "were you so consciously dear to me as now. I think of you hourly. Why then, you will ask, did I leave you? Because the love of Christ and perishing souls constrained me."

Referring in another place to the voyage, he says, "Many an hour, both by day and by night, was spent by me in pensive revery. The *past* filled my thoughts. Memory wandered alternately among flowers and graves."

CHAPTER VI.

Studies—Sailor Converted—Terrible Storm and Narrow Escape—Gratitude—Alone, yet not alone—At Java—Sights and Scenes—Missions of the Middle Ages.

"May 17. I have now mastered the two hundred and fourteen radicals, which may be regarded as in some sense the Chinese alphabet. I congratulate myself, therefore, on having advanced one step toward the acquisition of that most difficult of all difficult languages. I hardly dare attempt another step without the guidance of a teacher, lest I go wrong. I shall at least, from choice as well as necessity, follow the advice of the old Latin motto, '*Festina lente.*'

"May 22. Finished Smith's 'Researches in China;' and, on the whole, derive encouragement from his plain but interesting narrative. Little, indeed, has yet been accomplished; and so has it been in the early history of other missions, whose subsequent success has surprised and delighted the whole Christian world. When the set time to favor Zion in China comes, we know not what wonders of grace may be exhibited. Happy shall I be, if I may but clear away a little of the rubbish, which has been accumulating there for centuries, in preparation for the erection of a spiritual temple, where God shall be worshiped in ages to come. I often feel like putting my hand to the work, not with a romantic, but with an *enthusiastic* spirit.

"May 27. I enjoy the hours set apart for direct communion with God, more and more. Heaven and the holy objects therein, are becoming, more than ever before, all in all to me. Not that I am impatiently awaiting the termination of my earthly toils and sufferings. I am willing to bear the burden and heat of the day, all my allotted time; but then, how I shall welcome the hour of full discharge! How gladly shall I ascend to the presence of my God, and to the perfection of his saints.

"May 28. In thinking of my future work in China, I have been comforted with the reflection that Bible Christianity is to be inculcated, and not American Theology. How simple a thing the gospel is, adapted to every grade of intellect. How admirable the manner in which Christ impressed the truth upon his auditors. Fifty modern treatises on Theology are not so useful to a missionary as one of the New Testament parables. There is certainly little mystery or difficulty in the apostolical precept, 'Believe in the Lord Jesus Christ, and thou shalt be saved.' All can understand it, all may obey it.

"June 11. This evening had personal conversation with two of the sailors. One of them seems to be very near the kingdom of heaven. On inquiring at the outset, "How do you feel now in regard to this subject;' his reply was, 'Miserable! miserable!' I tried to direct him to the Lamb of God, that taketh away the sin of the world. He seemed to feel all that was said; but pleaded the difficulties in the way of living a Christian life in the forecastle. Poor fellow! I pity him, but his duty is plain. I told him he must be willing to suffer for Christ's sake. Oh, that he may be brought savingly to Jesus.

"June 15. This evening the sailor mentioned, expresses the hope that he has given himself to Christ, and has been accepted. This will greatly encourage us in our further labors among the crew. I have tried to give him such advice as I thought would be most serviceable to him. God grant that he may not be permitted to rest in a deception.

"June 23. A fit of industry which recently seized me, has resulted in leading me to devote my evenings, as well as mornings to the study of Chinese. At present I am reading, in order, Williams' Vocabulary; a dry, but I trust, not unprofitable task. It renders me familiar with the characters, and gives me an insight into the structure and genius of the language. No secular occupation affords me more real pleasure than this, uninviting as it may appear at first view. I would fain hope that the love of Christ sweetens this toil, and every other, which has for its object the salvation of men and the glory of God.

"July 3, Monday. 'Bless the Lord, O my soul, and all that is within me bless his holy name!' Such is the utterance of my heart in reviewing the last two days. We have been in imminent danger of shipwreck, and yet been mercifully delivered. The storm, which commenced on Saturday, increased in fury until last night at dusk.

It was made up of a succession of squalls, with intervals of comparative calm. Almost every squall was accompanied by hail. The sky was clear, directly over head, a considerable part of the time, while dense masses of cloud rested on the horizon all around. The sea, raised to a fearful height, broke over the quarter deck continually, threatening to sweep the helmsman from his post. The barometer stood at 29.05. We scudded under close-reefed topsails and reefed foresails, till last evening about five o'clock, when we shipped a huge sea, which passed over the boat, carried away a large part of the monkey rail, stove the galley-door, and set adrift the scuttle-butt, hen coops, spars and the like.

"Knowing that a few more such seas would wreck us, the captain concluded to heave to, which he did under close-reefed main-topsail. This done he entered with the remark, 'Everything now depends on the good qualities of the vessel; if she ships a sea, it is all over with her.' Our gallant little bark behaved nobly, however, and rode like a sea-bird amid the hills and the valleys of water. She seemed like a thing of life, struggling with a thousand furies, which hissed and shrieked around her.

"I was in momentary expectation of death during part of the time; but, through grace, I felt no fear of what was to follow. My sins rose to view, but I was able to look from them to Him who taketh away the sin of the world. It was a pleasing reflection in those hours that I had at least proposed to be a missionary. I rejoiced that I had come thus far on my way to preach the gospel among pagans. I trust the Lord has a great work for me to perform in China, and that he is sparing me that I may finish it. Oh, may I henceforth be more entirely his, both in life and in death.

"July 9. The sailor previously mentioned is still giving us encouraging evidence that a radical change is progressing, if not already wrought, in his character.

"July 17. The following lines are the product of a pensive hour this evening."

ALONE, YET NOT ALONE.

Alone I run the race of life,
And haste to reach its goal;
No kindred spirit by my side,
To cheer my fainting soul.

Alone I heave the mournful sigh
And shed the bitter tear;
No friend to share the bounding joy,
Or check the rising fear.

Alone I trace sad memory's page,
Where lives the happy past;
Weeping the early death of hope,
Too sweet, too bright, to last.

Alone I bow my knees in prayer
At morn, at noon, at night;
For wife or child no more I plead,—
They walk the realms of light.

Alone? no! distant be the thought,
While Christ my Saviour lives;
He knows each pang which rends my heart,
My weakness he forgives.

Alone I need not be in life,
Nor yet in death's dread hour;
O, Jesus! keep me near thy side,
Uphold me by thy power!

"July 20. About half past five this afternoon, the joyful cry, Land ho! was heard from the fore-top-sail yard, where one of the sailors was at work; and soon all eyes were directed to Java Head, which loomed up in the distance, like a pile of cumulus clouds. It is just one hundred days since our eyes were resting on the heights of Neversink, at the entrance of New York Bay. The evening was spent in a considerably excited state of feeling by all on board, the officers being busy in identifying the different heights which successively appeared, and the passengers in alternately gazing out on the dusky landscape, and penning a few lines for home. How grateful should we be to Him who has protected us thus far, amid all the dangers of our watery way; who has kept us from sickness, and given us prosperous winds. O Lord, let thy care still be over us; bring us to our destined port; and prepare us to be eminently useful among the heathen.

"July 21. Long before sunrise this morning, I was on deck gazing delightedly on the scene spread around. Java lay on the one hand, and Sumatra on the other; the former distinctly revealed in the gray dawn, the latter distant and shadowy. The sun rose magnificently from among the mountain summits, gilding with his beams the sky, the sea, the shore. Oh, thought I, could the glorious Sun of righteousness thus illuminate these islands, what Edens they might become. Silently did my prayer ascend to God, that their wretched inhabitants might soon become acquainted with the way of salvation through a crucified Saviour.

"Soon after sunrise we observed a native boat approaching us, and in a few moments four Malays were on our deck. Their only clothing was a cloth extending from the waist to the knee, and a sort of turban on the head. As we slowly advanced toward our anchorage at Anjier Point, boat after boat came alongside; all filled with swarthy natives, and the productions of the island, including bananas, yams, oranges, mangosteens, cocoanuts, parrots, Java sparrows, monkeys, and several curious kinds of little animals. The owners of these various articles displayed consummate tact, both in bargaining and begging. The boats were most of them, like the canoes of some Indian tribes, made by hollowing out a single log. The apparatus for steering was primitive, but ingenious.

"We cast anchor at twelve o'clock, about a quarter of a mile from the Dutch Fort. The Captain gave us an invitation to go ashore with him, which we of course eagerly accepted, both for the purpose of leaving our letters and seeing the novelties. Immediately on landing, an official with bare-legs and a drawn sword escorted us into the presence of the Governor, who lives in a comfortable house not far from the wharf. We made our way thither among crowds of natives, some of whom were busy and many of whom were idle. The Governor received us with great cordiality, the Captain and himself being old acquaintances. There we heard respecting the insurrection in China and the war in Europe to the date of 24th of May. Moreover, we had the opportunity of refusing a glass both of wine and of gin. In reply to our inquiries, the Governor assured us that the Island contained a population of more than ten millions; and, what was matter of greater surprise to us, that a single person unarmed might travel throughout its whole extent without the fear of molestation; and that too, (to pile wonder on wonder,) even if it were known that he carried with him thousands of dollars! The apartments were large and the ceilings very high. Numbers of servants were passing back and forth.

"We next proceeded to the house of the Javanese merchant from whom our Captain always procures his supplies, where we found a table set out with refreshments for us. Rarely have I enjoyed a lunch more. There were piled up on numerous small dishes, oranges, mangosteens, bananas, several kinds of little cakes, and a something which looked and tasted like cocoanut-candy. Tea and English ale were the potables. While addressing ourselves to these viands, the door was crowded with lookers on, and some even pressed into the room for a nearer view, all which seemed to be no violation of Javanese etiquette. One of the wives of our host was present, (he has two,) and his only child, a boy four or five years old, was playing about the floor naked.

"With a native boy as a guide, we next visited the fort, which is garrisoned by forty-five European soldiers, besides some native troops. Everything here seemed to be in good order, though an English ship of the line would soon spoil the beauty of the walls and embankments. We called on the Doctor to whom we were directed, with a view to ascertain whether there was a resident Chaplain. He received us as if we had been old friends, and with the aid of three languages, English, German and Latin, we managed to carry on quite a lively conversation. From him we learned that religious services were performed only once in three months, by a clergyman who came for that purpose from Batavia.

On leaving the fort, our guide conducted us to a fine cocoanut grove not far distant, by a path lined with the luxuriant vegetation of the tropics. The cocoanut trees are set out in regular rows, and are loaded with fruit in all stages of growth, from the forming nut to that which is fully ripe. After returning to the village we joined the captain and proceeded to the Mohammedan Mosque. The door was open, and we entered. The building was square, rising in the centre to a point. The floor was of stone or plaster, partly covered with mats. On the right and left of the door were suspended two drums of enormous size, which are probably used to summon the faithful to their orisons. The pulpit had very much the appearance, and the relative position, of the pulpit in most American Episcopal Churches. Conspicuous in the back of it were two apertures of crescent form, the symbol of that delusive faith. How strange that an island so remote should be devoted to the false prophet! Shame on Christians who are so indifferent to the progress of Christ's cause among men! On leaving the building, we noticed two pools of water, which are doubtless for the ablutions of the worshipers.

"Before returning to the ship, Mr. B. and myself strolled down one of the long streets, everywhere admiring nature, and pitying man. Coming unexpectedly upon the market place, we passed back and forth among its stalls, many of which were loaded with the betel nut in some form. Scarcely did we meet an individual in all our wanderings whose red lips did not betray the use of this article. This practice, and that of filing and blackening the teeth, give to the mouths of all a hideous appearance, rendering positively ugly many a face which might otherwise be pleasing.

"A short detention at the wharf while the boat was got in readiness, afforded us a fine opportunity for contemplating the scene. We sat down under an immense banyan tree, supported by more than a hundred trunks, all, however, uniting to form one. These trunks, instead of being at some distance from each other, formed a mass, more or less compact, in the centre of the spreading foliage which they bore. Large numbers of natives were scattered about; some passing fruits into the boats near by, some bathing, some selling cooked rice, some digging holes for a fence with sharp bamboo sticks, some making ropes, some begging, some idly looking on. We reached the vessel just before dark, glad to escape from the heat and confusion on land, yet charmed with our first walk on a tropical shore.

"My experience in Java, however, is not yet all recounted. During the entire evening the sound of music was borne to our ears by the land-breeze, accompanied by other noises of revelry. On making inquiry we were informed by some of the natives who yet remained on board, that the inhabitants were engaged in a dance, which would be kept up till after midnight. The captain resolved to go on shore to see the sight, and I concluded to accompany him.

"The market-place was now the ball-room, lighted by a number of lamps of primitive construction. There were three separate companies of musicians and dancers. The musicians in each case occupied the elevated platform on which the various wares had been displayed during the day, while the dancers performed on the ground in front. Each 'band' has four instruments; one a long drum, which was struck with the hands, and resembled in sound the same instrument at home; another a huge gong; the third a two-stringed fiddle; and the fourth a nondescript article, which looked as much like three iron pots, standing side by side, with covers of like material, as anything else. These covers were beaten with two drum-sticks.

"Three dancing girls stood in front, ready for any partners who might offer; nor were they ever compelled to wait long. A man would emerge from the surrounding gloom, with a cloth thrown over his head and hanging down over his shoulders, take his place in front, and commence the performance. Both sexes were half naked, and the little clothing they had on was singularly arranged. Both musicians and dancers accompanied the instruments with the most horrible perversions of the human voice to which I ever listened. Strange to say, though the captain and myself were the only whites amid this mass of half savage Malays, nothing disrespectful to us was said or done. I can remember, but not describe, my sensations, as I stood near the dancers, now gazing on their half-frenzied movements, now on the swarthy faces and forms of the natives who pressed against me in the crowd, and now out into the gloomy shadows of the surrounding trees.

"We were rowed to the ship by natives in a native boat, reaching it at one o'clock, A. M. Wearied with my walks, and worn out by the heat, I threw myself on the bed and slept soundly till morning.

"July 22. Weighed anchor about ten o'clock, and with a hardly perceptible breeze, stood away from Anjier. I almost experienced a feeling of regret as the beautiful landscape faded from my sight. Nothing is wanting but the gospel to transform Java into an earthly Eden. I no longer wonder that the early navigators among the South Sea Islands found it difficult to keep their crews from abandoning the ship. The life which a European might lead among these primitive people just suits the natural heart. The means of subsistence can be procured with little trouble, and the face of nature ever wears a smile.

"July 28. Much interested yesterday and to-day in reading Neander's 'Sketches from the History of Missions in the Middle Ages.' Truly, although these are justly denominated the 'dark ages,' many *individuals* in the church were burning and shining lights. Some seem to have been both superstitious and pious; in bondage to an ascetic spirit, and yet free in Christ Jesus. I find much in the character of these holy men, and indeed much in their conduct, well worthy of imitation; particularly their readiness to suffer for Christ, their strong and simple faith, and their perseverance in the midst of discouragements."

CHAPTER VII.

Arives at Hong Kong—Voyage up the Coast—Typhoon—At Shanghai—The City and Suburbs—In the hands of Rebels—Begins Missionary work—Studies and Obstacles.

ON the 5th of August, 1854, the missionaries reached Hong Kong. Of their brief stay among hospitable brethren in that city and their subsequent perilous voyage up the coast, Mr. Aitchison speaks very freely in the following extract from a letter written one week after reaching Shanghai.

[To C. P. B.]

"SHANGHAI, *September* 7, 1854.

* * * * "Arriving at Hong Kong, we were most cordially received by Rev. Mr. Johnson of the American Baptist Board, and by Rev. Dr. Legge and Rev. Mr. Chalmers of the London Missionary Society. At the house of the latter brethren we spent a fortnight very pleasantly. Such was the troubled state of Canton, (now be-

sieged by the rebels,) that we did not deem it advisable to visit that city. You cannot imagine how strangely everything strikes one on his first arrival in such a country as China. One can hardly feel that he is the same being who not long before was in such different circumstances.

"Hong Kong is a barren, hilly spot, without shrubs or trees, except those planted by the hand of man. Victoria, the British settlement, contains a population of more than thirty thousand. It is not regarded as a promising missionary station, because it is the resort of the lowest class of the natives.

"On Saturday morning, August 19th, we sailed from Hong Kong for Shanghai, in the ship '*James Booth.*' Being compelled the first night to cast anchor among some small islands, we loaded our two cannon and our muskets, and kept a double watch till morning. These warlike preparations were demanded by the great numbers of pirates at present infesting these China waters.

"When just emerging from the Formosa Straits, we encountered a Typhoon, which lasted just two days, and came very near wrecking us. We knew that we must be near land, and feared every

Chinese Junk.

Five Years in China. P. 92.

hour, especially in the darkness, that we should find ourselves close on a lee shore. The sublimity of such a storm on the ocean surpasses all that a landsman can conceive. The wind blows with a fury which seems at times absolutely irresistible. And then such a *sea!* Our fore-yards dipped into the crests of the billows! The largest vessel, noble an object as she is, seems like a poor, helpless thing in such circumstances. God was with us however, as a protector and preserver. We escaped without suffering any damage, except a few bruised limbs of sailors who were thrown over the wheel.

"We set foot in Shanghai on the afternoon of September 1st, and received a cordial, Christian welcome from Rev. Dr. Bridgman and wife, and from the whole missionary company. It was a real pleasure to lie down at night, secure from all the dangers of the deep, without a thought as to how the wind blows or the sky looks. I trust some proper feelings of gratitude to God filled my heart, when I thought of the long way in which I had been kindly led, and the many dangers from which I had been delivered."

Shanghai is a city of nearly 150,000 inhabitants, perhaps 200,000 with the suburbs. It is the most northerly and most important of the five ports which were opened to foreigners by the treaty of 1842. It is in the latitude of Southern Georgia, in this country, although of a much colder climate. It is surrounded by a vast and fertile plain, rich in products such as rice, wheat, barley, cotton, and teeming with a busy population. Its harbor sometimes contains three thousand vessels and junks, all swarming with human beings, a city afloat, while its communications and trade by water alone extend to one third part of the whole empire. There was in this city a number of missionaries of other denominations; and Rev. Mr. Bridgman, who was the first missionary of the American Board to China, having gone out in 1830, and who had been stationed at Canton, had been residing in Shanghai for several years, and in connection with a committee of the several missions, was engaged in revising and perfecting the translation of the Holy Scriptures; but as yet the American Board had no established mission in this important city. Mr. Aitchison and Mr. Blodget were to begin one. But first, Mr. Aitchison makes his safe arrival the occasion of a solemn thanksgiving to God for all his mercies in the past, for protection and comfort in the long and perilous voyage; and then still more solemnly consecrates himself anew to the service of his Divine Master, and especially to all the toils and trials of his contemplated missionary life, praying fervently for divine guidance and help in his holy calling.

The city, on the arrival of the missionaries, was in the hands of a band of local banditti, a part of the great rebellion, who held it in the face of thousands of imperial troops for about a year and a half, with no little annoyance, inconvenience, and sometimes danger, to the foreign residents.

It is here, in the midst of this confusion, and these troubles, that Mr. Aitchison begins his missionary life. We have seen how God led him by that mysterious way which his own thoughts could never have marked out, to make him a "chosen vessel" unto himself; and we shall now see the sanctified fruit of that baptism of sorrow which his soul had received.

The following is from the letter of Sept. 7th, to which we have before referred:—

"The city is still in the hands of the insurgents, and is likely to be till dooms-day for aught the Imperialists can do. The war as it is carried on here is mainly a farce. Skirmishing goes on at any hour of the day or night; and indeed there is hardly an hour in which you do not hear the booming of cannon. All last night

> 'We heard the distant and random gun,
> Which the foe were sullenly firing.'

Even while the Imperial troops are engaged in bombarding the city, the residents are attending to their daily business about as usual.

"Of course such a state of things is unfavorable to the successful prosecution of missionary labors, so far as the *city* is concerned. But hundreds of thousands in the country around are accessible. I wish you could have accompanied me last Sunday in the distribution of tracts. Everywhere we were kindly received. Our books were eagerly sought for; and a new comer would suppose that the people were hungering for the bread of life. There appeared to be a wonderful readiness on the part of the people to receive the truth. But alas! the experience of the missionaries proves that such appearances are deceitful. Of the thousands of books and tracts distributed, few have ever been heard from."

On the very day after his arrival in Shanghai, with the aid of a native teacher, Mr. Aitchison entered upon the more exact and systematic study of the Chinese language. With the three hours a day so scrupulously devoted to this study during a large portion of the voyage he had already made an ample beginning; but now, by the help of the living teacher, and frequent intercourse with the people, he is enabled to make more rapid progress; so that he commenced preaching in that most difficult of all languages, in just one year from the day of taking that first oral lesson. We shall see in the end what distinguished attainments he made in five years. At the very commencement of his course also, he thus indicated his choice amid the many departments of missionary labor, and his consequent line of study.

"My present plan of procedure is to make myself familiar with the spoken language of the Chinese, and to present the offer of salvation through Christ to as many individuals as possible.

I design to spend my life in *preaching;* leaving *teaching*, except in the gospel sense, to others. To carry out my plan with any degree of success requires, of course, an accurate knowledge of the medium of oral communication. To the acquisition of the language, therefore, I must devote all my energies for some time to come."

In his journal of Sept. 2d he thus describes his first lesson:

"This forenoon we took our first lesson in Chinese. We were left alone in a room with a teacher, whom Dr. Bridgman had engaged for us. The commencement of my studies was sufficiently awkward and embarrassing to all parties. We could only point to various objects around us and *look* the question, 'What is that called?' We are, however, encouraged by our friends to hope that in a single year we may be able to converse quite fluently on common topics."

In a letter of Sept. 14th, Mr. Aitchison says:

"Our chief attention for the present is given to the Shanghai *colloquial.* The Mandarin, or Court dialect, or more properly the general language of the country, is a separate affair alto gether."

The journal of Sept. 2d thus portrays the hapless condition of the beleaguered town:

"In the afternoon we went into the city proper, partly to see the ground belonging to our mission, partly to smuggle out some clothes belonging to our teacher, and partly to see the novelties of the place. While passing through one of the streets, we met a small company of mounted rebel troops. They were a sorry-looking set, only half armed, and some of them little more than half dressed. Just outside the walls, ruins frowned upon us everywhere, the dire effects of former conflicts. Within the gates, which are carefully guarded, we were everywhere treated with the greatest respect, the very children saluting us with the honorary title, '*sien sang*,' (teacher.) The Imperialists are encamped on all sides of the city, but thus far all their efforts to get possession of it have failed.

"Sept. 3, Sabbath. The Lord's Supper was administered to-day in the London mission chapel. How pleasant to have the privilege of thus celebrating the Saviour's love on the first Sabbath after our arrival. A sweet peace filled my soul, which was only made deeper and sweeter by the distant booming of cannon, which came from the opposing armies. On returning to the house we saw from the verandah the balls bounding across the water, between the imperial battery and the rebel fortifications. Some of the missionaries here have had their houses repeatedly struck by shot during the last year. But God has graciously protected them, and allowed no harm to befall them. What is to be the progress and result of this insurrection, no man can foresee. We cannot but believe that God will bring great good to his people and kingdom out of all this apparent evil.

"Sept. 10. Enjoyed the presence of God to some extent to-day. At nine o'clock I went to the Chinese service, conducted by our Episcopal brethren, and heard what I presume was a faithful sermon. Was astonished and gratified to see so large an audience—between two and three hundred. This number includes two or three schools. The children looked neat, clean and happy. After service my teacher came to my room, and read to me, in Chinese, the first twelve verses of the 5th chapter of Matthew. Oh, how I longed to be able to communicate to him my ideas on the great subject of salvation. I could only point to the sixth verse, and by signs intimate to him that I hoped he would take the matter into serious consideration. He has been employed for a long time as a teacher in missionary families, and is well acquainted with the doctrines of Christianity. I learn that he is a candidate for baptism. Oh, that the Holy Spirit would make him a true disciple, and employ him as an instrument in enlightening his countrymen.

"Spent three hours or more in distributing books among the inhabitants of the various hamlets scattered through the rice fields to the north of the city. This may be regarded as my first missionary effort in China. We were everywhere welcomed and treated with politeness. Our books were almost snatched from our hands by the people, so eager were they to get possession of them.

"Our path led through rice and cotton fields interspersed everywhere with graves and coffins. We passed a company of mourners, making lamentation at a tomb, all dressed in white, which is the mourning color. Mr. Cabaniss accompanied us, and conversed with the people. Many seemed to be acquainted with the name of the Saviour.

"Ya-soo'—Jesus. Some readily confessed their ignorance in reference to the state of the soul after death. All listened with apparent interest to what was said, but some question directly foreign to the subject in hand would betray the real direction of their thoughts."

In a letter of Sept. 14th, again he writes:—"Shanghai is still in a very unsettled state. The Imperial troops are encamped about it, and battles are affairs of constant occurrence. Yesterday afternoon we went to call upon some missionary families who live not far from the city wall, and near the camp of the Imperialists. As we were approaching their residence, the thunder of artillery and the sight of smoke not far distant somewhat startled us. We went on however, and from the verandah of Brother Carpenter's house we had a view of the battle-field, less than a mile distant. The Imperialists were just retreating in good order to their camp. We saw their long lines fairly fluttering in the breeze, for without exaggeration about every tenth man carries a banner. The rebels were firing at them from the walls. There had been quite a smart engagement in the forenoon, and in passing across the fields to the house of Brother Cunnyngham, we saw a man lying dead by the road-side. He had been killed by a stray ball while looking on. Coming to the door of Mr. C's. house, we counted in it six marks of balls; and he informed us that the house had been hit more than forty times within the last year. Proceeding a little further to the house of Brother Yates, we found it *riddled* with balls; and yet there he resides with his wife, for he cannot find another place where to lay his head.

"You will be ready to ask if the missionaries do not feel that their lives are in danger. The most of us are in no special peril; only those who reside near the wall need feel anxiety. The relations sustained by the missionaries, and by the foreign community in general, to the belligerents are complicated and curious. The territory occupied by foreigners is really under martial law. The 'three powers,' English, French and American furnish each a regular guard, who are stationed at certain points to prevent any armed Chinamen from setting foot on their territory. It is said that yesterday the two armies, while fighting, encroached somewhat on the neutral ground, when a few English marines fired into them, causing their immediate flight, one part to the city, and the other to their camp.

"The obstacles to the success of missionary efforts in China are many and peculiar. When we survey the desolations around us, and then think of our own weakness, we should assuredly fold our hands in utter despair did we not remember that Christ lives, and that all power is given to him in heaven and on earth. This great empire is surely a part of that world which is to be full of the knowledge of the Lord, as the waters cover the sea. Jesus has both the power and the disposition to secure the interests and the progress of his own kingdom. It does not become us then to be painfully anxious on these points, except so far as they are connected with our own faithfulness. Though we who are now in the field may labor on till death, uncheered by a single ray of success, yet we believe our lives will not have been in vain. God will graciously accept our efforts; yea, he will make them conducive to the future triumph of his gospel in this benighted land. And we, from our mansions of rest may be permitted to witness the progress of the chariot of salvation along the path which we had a hand in preparing."

CHAPTER VIII.

The number of the people—No Sabbath—Chinese Funeral—Excursion with Rev. Mr. Edkins—Stopped by officials at Soo-Chow—Sent back under escort.

THUS the young missionary entered upon his labors, not over-confident in himself, but looking to the right source for help. The following extract from his first letter to the American Board still further shows how formidable the work appears to his first vision of it.

"One thing which struck me forcibly at first, and continues to be a matter of daily wonder, is the number of the people. They congregate everywhere. The streets are thronged; the houses are crowded; the boats in the river are overflowing. You can find no retired spot, out of your own house, where you may go forth, to walk, like Isaac, and 'meditate at eventide.' Take what direction you please, and penetrate as far as you will into the country, you will find thickly inhabited hamlets, and be jostled by bustling passers-by. Mr. Poor, when in America, truly remarked that the human race is located in the east. It is painful to mingle daily in these crowds of perishing men, and yet be speechless.

"In connection with this point come thoughts of the magnitude of the work to be accomplished, and the inadequacy of the means now employed. How are these masses to be reached and impressed? How can their deeply rooted pride and prejudice be removed? What is to loosen their attachment to systems of error long since hoary with age? How can they be brought to accept a cross-bearing religion, taught by those whom they despise? And how is all this to be brought to pass through the medium of the most impracticable language spoken by man? We might despair, were we compelled to rely on the number or the wisdom of human instrumentalities. But with God all things are possible. He is wonderful in counsel and excellent in working. Even now events seem to be looking toward a crisis, which may herald the day of China's redemption."

The following brief observations from Mr. A's. journal present matters of interest.

Oct. 7. He writes, "I am in great danger of losing my compassion for the people by mingling with them without the power of labouring for them. The sensibilities become blunted; the mind becomes accustomed to the contemplation of ignorance and misery. O God keep my heart tender! let me not forget that every individual of these multitudes has an immortal soul to be saved or lost. Let nothing damp my ardor or diminish my zeal.

"Oct. 8. The Sabbath. There is no Sabbath here. Everything among the Chinese population goes on as usual. That sacred stillness of a New England Sabbath, almost forcing the soul to pious meditation, is wholly wanting. Trade, gambling and labor are engaged in as on ordinary days. Oh, when will China rest on the Lord's day, and repair to the sanctuary to worship him in the beauty of holiness! Hasten thy coming, O Lord!

"Dec. 24. Saw to-day a long procession at the funeral rites of a man of wealth. There were boys with flags, men with huge gongs, priests with gay robes, musicians and mourners dressed in white, all wearing an air of exceeding jollity, perhaps in anticipation of the good things which were borne on the shoulders of men, such as a whole hog roasted, a sheep ditto, and several large dishes of fruit and cakes. Oh, the exceeding folly of idolatry in all its doctrines and practices! The ceremonies connected with the worship of the gods here in China would be as amusing as a farce, were they not sinful and soul-destroying. Talked once or twice to a few people. Would that my tongue were loosed, and then touched with a live coal from off the altar."

In the month of January, in company with Rev. Mr. Edkins, of the London Missionary Society, Mr. Aitchison undertook an excursion "towards" the interior. It was intended as a tour of observation, with efforts to do good wherever they should go. They started on the morning of the 16th of the month, and at nightfall Mr. Aitchison wrote:

"How strange to be here! Thirty-five miles west of Shanghai, in the Empire of China! Who would have predicted this two years and a half ago? Truly, it is not in man that walketh to direct his steps. O Lord, here, in this new place, in these strange circumstances, I give myself anew to thee. Make me an instrument of good among this people, and fit me for thy will and kingdom."

On the 17th they visited "Long Water" Pagoda. "The principal priest," says Mr. Aitchison, "who waited upon us, was a man of venerable aspect and considerable urbanity. When Mr. E. was here four years ago he was confined in a small room in fulfillment of a vow, which for some reason had been made. In conversation he advocated the refined notions of the sect to which he belongs, in reference to the nonexistence of all external things, going even beyond Bishop Berkeley in the process of etherialization. Strange that a people like the Chinese, of all men most practical, should have a religion of all on earth most metaphysical. The Budhist speculations seem to annihilate every thing—nature, the soul, and even God himself."

In this journey the missionaries sailed through a succession of lakes and rivers, passing a constant series of large towns and villages, suffering not a little with the cold by day and by night, the boatmen sometimes breaking the ice in the streams, as they pushed their boat along.

Chinese Pagoda.

Five Years in China. P. 110.

On the 18th Mr. Aitchison wrote,—"As we advanced, I could not but take notice of the immense number of people engaged in fishing, and the numberless methods they employ to entrap their finny prey. Sometimes a man with one hand is able to manage the apparatus, while at others a number of men have to exert all their strength. Many of the fish taken and carried to market are exceedingly small, such as a home fisherman would not think it worth while to look at. Great numbers of wild ducks and other birds are seen everywhere, and they manifest but little fear of men."

"Jan. 19. Soon after breakfast we came to the famous *Grand Canal*, which is an enduring memorial of the enterprise and energy of a former age."

Thus the missionaries passed on their way, preaching and distributing books wherever they went, until they came near the great city of Suchau. Here, as Mr. Aitchison says, their "misfortunes began;" and of these the journal contains so graphic and interesting an account, that we copy it entire.

"Going on shore at a village, leaving our boat

to follow, we passed on to the other side, when, casting our eye to the left, we saw the tri-cornered flag floating at the top of a spear, the sure proof of a military post. Before we had time for a moment's reflection, the petty officer was at our side, inviting us, in a most polite manner, to a seat in the building. We looked anxiously for our boat, but it was not in sight, and we could do nothing but accept the invitation. In a few moments we rose to go, but were, in the same extremely polite manner, informed that the higher officer wished to see us.

"By this time numbers of soldiers, petty officers, and a great crowd of people, surrounded us. We saw that we were in an awkward predicament, so we quietly resolved to make the best of it. Being escorted to the other side, we were conducted to a temple, where we were introduced to a mandarin of the lower grade, his rank being indicated by a white ball on his cap. He inquired where we were from, and whither we were going. We told him from Shanghai, and to Choong-loong San, and that our present object was to visit the pagoda, in the mountains near by. He was very gracious; answered that he would

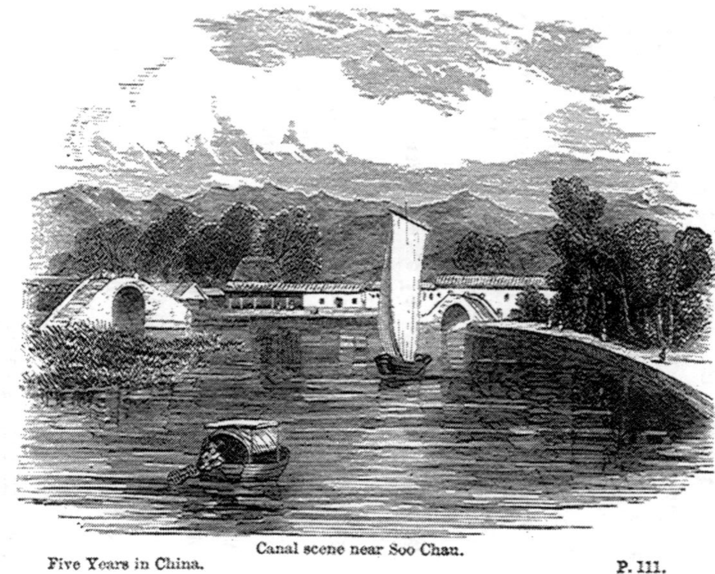

Canal scene near Soo Chau.

Five Years in China. P. 111.

be happy to render us assistance, and that in order to do this, it would be necessary to conduct us to Suchau, where we might obtain leave from his superior. After that, he himself would accompany us on our proposed ramble.

"This proposal to take us to Suchau was what we most dreaded, but there was of course no remedy. Numbers of troops were now gathered around us; some of them with long spears, and some with naked swords in their hands. While our mandarin friend was getting his boat ready, we made good use of our time by distributing a great number of books among the soldiers and the crowd. There was a tremendous rush for them, insomuch that we were almost afraid to proceed, lest the people, in their eagerness, should push each other into the water. All was, however, soon ready, and we started, the mandarin in his boat, and we in ours, attended by five or six well armed soldiers. As our boat was a fast sailer, we soon got far ahead of his, and took the opportunity to have a fine walk on shore, in the suburbs of the far-famed city.

"One thing which struck me here was the display of earthen ware, particularly the huge jars so universally used throughout China. They were stacked up in all imaginable forms, and in heaps of all dimensions. On entering our boat again we distributed a large number of books.

"After passing great numbers of huge junks, such as are employed in carrying grain to Peking, we reached the West gate of Suchau, and landing, immediately entered within the walls. We were conducted at a rapid pace to the premises of the officer in command of the militia, a mandarin wearing a crystal ball. While the dignitaries were holding a short consultation together, we were the centre of attraction to a large crowd who had by this time gathered around us. In a few minutes a messenger summoned us to the presence of the crystal ball, when we underwent a sort of cross-examination, Mr. Edkins, being of course, here, and throughout the narrative, the only speaker.

"The result of these interrogations was an expression of friendship on the mandarin's part, and a professed willingness to favor our object, *but* it did not lie in his power to decide in the case. Accordingly we were to be sent to the chief magistrate of the city, to await his pleasure.

Chinese Noblemen in consultation.

Five Years in China. P. 114.

Thither we were accordingly carried in chairs provided for the purpose, and as our route lay through one or two of the crowded thoroughfares, we had a fair opportunity to see the shops and the people. There was a great display of fruits, including large fine-looking apples. Two soldiers with huge swords preceded, and two followed our chairs. At the gate of the Magistrate's office, a great rabble awaited our arrival, many of whom followed us within.

"Here, in an anteroom, which was low, dark and dirty, we awaited the decision of the functionary. It soon came, and with it the disappointment of our hopes respecting a sight of Choong-Loong-San. We were to be conducted back to Shanghai immediately. Mr. E. argued the case at considerable length with the bearer of the decree, but argument was vain. We returned to the military office as we came, the streets being now lined on both sides by people eager to have a good look at the foreign barbarians. It was almost dark when we arrived, and after a few minutes' detention we were escorted to our boats through some bye-ways, first declining an urgent invitation to remain for dinner. Meanwhile our boats had been brought within the walls, so that we had the privilege of passing the night in Suchau. A present of eatables accompanied us, consisting of mutton, and a sort of meat pies, in common use among the Chinese.

"Jan. 20. This morning we rose early and took a walk for a quarter of a mile or more on the city wall. It was in good repair. At short intervals there were piles of rough stones, ready to be cast down on the heads of any enemies who might attempt to scale it. By the time we had reached our boat, one of the guard appointed to watch us was awake, and, attended by him, we strolled to a considerable distance along one of the streets. Numbers of persons followed us, though there was little disturbance. Scarcely was our breakfast finished when we were summoned to the military office. We went, and there we spent the entire day, uncertain whether to consider ourselves as guests or prisoners. The Mandarin himself spent most of the day in our company, and was very courteous. We begged the privilege of visiting some of the celebrated localities of the city, a request which he steadily but politely refused, alleging as a reason the fear of disturbance from a crowd of people, particularly in these troublous times.

"We roamed at will through the gardens and apartments of his establishment, finding much to interest and amuse us. In the gardens were artificial ponds, and mountains of rock, vines, dwarf trees, all of the most fantastic forms. A number of birds in cages discoursed sweet music, and curious summer-houses were reached by zigzag bridges. Within the house there were many apartments connected by labyrinthine passages, and entered by curiously shaped *apertures*. Doors there were none, but simple screens or curtains separated one room from another. The walls were adorned with innumerable pictures, and scrolls covered with the written character. The tables groaned under flower-pots, curiously wrought vases, books containing pictures, and other nondescript articles of native manufacture. At least eight or nine clocks were scattered about, all of foreign make, and some highly ornamented.

"One thing on which the proprietor evidently set high value was a lithographic print of a female head and bust, such as adorn the windows of so many shops in America. There were numerous small tables for writing or tea-drinking. He asked many questions about foreign affairs, and while Mr. E. was answering them, I at his request tried my hand at drawing something for him. I made something in the shape of a rose-bush, a waterfall, a bridge, and a man-of-war, all of which he pronounced excellent, meanwhile Mr. E. was turning a verse of poetry into Chinese, and the success of his effort elicited high encomiums from all present.

"Numbers of persons during all this time were coming in to see us, all of whom were from the first classes of Chinese society. We saw the bowings and scrapings attending an introduction, and the way in which superiors and inferiors treat each other. Tea was served two or three times, accompanied by some foreign biscuit, stamped 'Haylock's Arrowroot.' Twice we were regaled with warm milk, which was a real treat. As the evening drew on we grew impatient, and our host was prevailed upon to let us depart without waiting for the next morning. We told him that the next day being our day of worship, we should be unwilling to set out. A dinner was provided, consisting of pheasants, mutton, eggs, and a roast of which the material was unknown. We managed the chopsticks to the best of our ability, but still our efforts to get the tempting morsels into our mouths drew good-natured smiles and jokes from the bystanders. Some seemed disposed to show us how the thing was done by actual experiment, but we would not give them the opportunity.

"Next followed an entertainment of a different nature. A ring was formed, and several of the soldiers exhibited their strength and skill in the use of their weapons. The first who performed, wielded a savage-looking instrument, half spear, half scythe, which he held in both hands. The next went through a sword exercise; and the third had a sort of chain about three feet long, having a handle at the end. All intended to show their manner of dealing with an enemy in close combat. They accordingly advanced and retreated, flourishing their weapons in all imaginable ways, now thrusting, now hewing, now striking, then cleaving. They moved with great agility, and seemed to be masters, each of his weapon. There they might have passed for what they fancied themselves, brave and formidable men, but recent history proves them to be, in general, cruel and cowardly.

"At the moment of our departure our host offered us two dollars(!) to pay our expenses to Shanghai. Of course we refused to take the money, and he had the good sense not to press it upon us. In a few minutes we had bidden good-bye, to high and low; and, attended by our escort, consisting of a small Mandarin and two or three followers, in a boat of their own, we had issued from the south gate. We breathed more freely as we turned our prow homeward, delivered as we were from the officious kindness of our pretended friends. The sun was near the horizon when we started, but it was ten o'clock before we had escaped from the throng of boats which filled the canals in the neighborhood of the city. We cast anchor for the night under the wall, having sailed along its whole length in two directions."

On the 24th of January, after an absence of eight days, the missionaries again reached Shanghai, having visited many important towns, and "distributed, in all, three thousand volumes and tracts, including portions of the Bible."

CHAPTER IX.

Recapture of the City—Horrible Scenes—Missionaries' houses riddled—Churches unharmed—Difficulties of the language—Heathenism—A new home.

THE recapture of the city of Shanghai by the Imperialists, after it had been eighteen months in the hands of the rebels, occurred on the 17th of February, 1855; that being the first day of the Chinese year. On the Monday following, (19th) Mr. Aitchison entered the gate to view the desolation. "Such a scene of horrors," he said, in a letter to the Board, "I never before witnessed. One half of the city was in ruins, including all the finest business streets. Here and there the corpse of an insurgent was lying disembowelled in the street, or charred amid the smoking ruins. The city wall in the neighborhood of the six gates was grim with blood-besmeared heads elevated on bamboo poles. Troops were dispersed in all directions, searching every nook and corner for fresh victims, and taking possession of everything that pleased their fancy.

"Some poor wretches were discovered hiding in coffins and in the bottom of wells. Happy was he who perished in the conflict on the first night, for he escaped the ingenious torture to which others were exposed. At the lowest estimate six hundred persons have been beheaded here in the past week. Many of them doubtless pay the just forfeit of their crimes, whilst some, it is to be presumed, are wholly innocent.

"The fall of the city is the result, not of Chinese bravery, but of French interference. The Triads would have laughed at their imperial opponents, had the latter been unsupported by foreign allies. Two or three months since some difficulty arose between a few French marines and a detachment of rebels. The latter fired on the former, wounding one man. After some unsuccessful attempts at negotiations, the French Admiral brought his war steamer and frigate into position and bombarded the city three separate times. Once he breached the wall and attempted to enter, but was repulsed with the loss of about twelve men, including the first officer of the frigate. He next took efficient measures to cut off all supplies, and the result has been narrated above. Such interference on his part is generally and loudly condemned. It is hinted that the Romish Missionaries are at the bottom of it, but of this no one can be certain.

"It is remarkable that the missionaries have suffered so little amid all these troubles. Though frequently exposed to danger, no one of them has been injured. Some of their houses are, indeed, so riddled with shot, that they are not worth repairing, and many are forced to leave their dwellings; but the governor of the province gave them eighteen thousand dollars, the estimated value of their property, and now several think of returning at once to their places, either within or near the city wall. The churches and chapels also, in the city, belonging to the various missions, have all been preserved, and preaching will be resumed in most of them immediately.

"Oh, that this may be the beginning of a new order of things, spiritual as well as political, in Shanghai! There are about seventy missionaries assembled at this point. Surely we may hope for good things in the time to come."

The following extracts from free and friendly letters contain touching allusions to scenes of the past, with some passages of rare interest in respect to the work then in hand:

[To L. R. A.]

"SHANGHAI, *Feb.* 1, 1855.

"MY DEAR L:—It is nearly half past nine o'clock. Bro. B. and myself have just united in our customary evening worship; but before retiring I am disposed to have a little chat with you. Your letter I found waiting my return from a short excursion into, or rather *towards*, the interior of China. * * * * You wrote in the early autumn; I reply amid the snows of February; and you will read this with the birds and flowers of summer around you. What a commentary on the flight of time!

"The weather has been quite New England-like, except that very little snow falls. These north-westers are fresh from the icy plains of Tartary, and have a habit of searching one's house and person that is by no means agreeable. It is a matter of rejoicing to us that we have this cold bracing winter to prepare us for the oppressive summer. We have hardly had five rainy days during these last five months, and yet the natural dampness of the soil is such that the ground is still quite moist.

"We hold on the even tenor of our way, giving all our strength to the work of acquiring the language. Study is in general pleasant, though I occasionally get discouraged in view of my slow progress. After mastering the colloquial, we have still the Mandarin and the book language, with which to *recreate* ourselves. The time from nine to twelve, and from three to five, each day, is spent with my teacher.

"I have not yet attempted much in the way of direct effort for the spiritual welfare of the people, on account of my inability to speak fluently. But I am at times conscience-smitten at the thought of my neglect; for with such motives to labor, it seems as though we should be willing to *stammer* out the message.

China is no small island in mid-ocean whose few inhabitants are destined to vanish before the face of an advancing civilization. Here are congregated under one government a third of the human race, with laws and institutions, arts and sciences, which date back almost to the flood. The Empire in some shape will exist for ages to come, whatever may be the result of the present revolution, and every blow struck for Christ will resound through coming centuries; every breath of influence for good will be felt more or less directly by millions of souls. Ought not those whom God has called hither, in view of this fact alone, to strain every nerve, and employ every power in the Master's service?

[To C. P. B.]

SHANGHAI, *March* 1, 1855.

MY VERY DEAR BROTHER:—* * * * "Nothing of much importance in my personal history has occurred since my last date. Study has been the order of the day, and sometimes of the night. One makes but slow progress in a language like this. All his previous attainments afford but little assistance; though previous discipline of mind is of course an important auxiliary. The *tones* are the grand difficulty. Sometimes ten or more different ideas are represented by the same letters of the English alphabet, the signification of the word or syllable depending wholly on a slight, and to our Western ears, hardly perceptible modulation of the voice.

"For example, the two letters *zz* (double z,) when pronounced give *thirty-five* separate senses, which the *tone* distinguishes. A nice ear and well formed organs of speech are therefore important to a missionary among the Chinese. And yet this should not hinder any man of fair or even moderate abilities from coming here to labor. Blessed be God, the gospel is simple. Its fundamental truths are easy of expression, and easy of comprehension. In a very short time a person may acquire enough of the language to preach *Christ and him crucified;* and it is surely not to be regretted that the *subtleties* of some divines will be long in finding their way into the theology of the future Chinese churches. * * * *

"Idolatry has apparently a very feeble hold on the affections or intellect of the masses in this land; but it is pitiable to think of their ignorance and misery; above all when we consider their prospects for eternity—such a stream of immortals flowing down, age after age, to the gloomy gates of perdition. Oh, is not the spectacle calculated to arouse every feeling and energy of a Christian soul! How little is the church doing to stay this tide—to roll back these dark waves of death!

"Such reflections as these would be well nigh maddening, were it not for the knowledge of God's wisdom and love. His plans are hastening to their accomplishment. These uttermost parts of the earth are to be the scenes of Christ's most wonderful triumphs before the latter day glory is fully realized. * * * * *

"Are the Ministers' meetings sustained with as much interest as ever? Oh, what would I give to be present at another! Those were golden hours. I often fancy I see you in your earnest discussions and friendly communings. The missionary's trials are not connected with food and raiment and dwelling. Oh, no! they arise in great part from the deprivation of Christian fellowship, from the little success attending his labors, and from a contemplation of the moral desolations around him. Commend me affectionately to all the brethren, and ask their prayers on my behalf.

"Do write me frequently, letters are so refreshing in this land of darkness. One sees almost nothing here which is pleasing. In fact, all the five senses are constantly offended; and the soul, of course, suffers in sympathy with them. All items of local news are welcome. Tell me what you do and see, where you go, what you are planning, and the like. Please give kind remembrances to all the Greeneville friends. *Ever faithfully yours.*"

[To L. R. A.]

"SHANGHAI, *March* 9, 1855.

"MY DEAR L:—I am sitting to-night in the new house, and in my own room. It is a luxury to have an apartment all to one's self. Please walk into my sanctum and take a seat. You see it resembles the sitting-room in the cottage, being thirteen feet by fourteen. Just at the left hand as you enter the door is the fire-place, in front of which stands the nice stove I brought with me from New York. On the mantel shelf is the drawing of New Haven Green, by my darling Mary, a silent but eloquent companion of my waking hours. Next comes a neat wash-stand with its furniture of blue China ware, occupying the place of your door opening into the back hall. Passing the window on the second side we come to my study-table, which is well loaded with apparatus for experimenting in the art of speech making. At each end is an armchair with fancy legs and back. On the third side stands a book-case well stocked, then a smaller one, (the gift of J. Y. L.; blessings on him!) then a trunk. Side number four presents for inspection an article of my own planning, which answers for a settee by day and a bed by night, quite a convenience in so small a room; then a table surmounted by a small mirror and well covered with books and daguerreotypes. Before the stove lies a large dog-skin mat, and in the centre of the room is the rocking-chair so sacred in my eyes.* The floor is covered with some Canton straw matting. So you see we are not destitute of comforts in China.

"Here I shall probably be located for at least six months to come. Here I shall muse many an hour over bye-gone years. Here I shall vainly long for spiritual communion with those who have entered the unseen world. Here I shall mourn over the moral condition of these

* That in which his beloved Mary died.

Chinese Gods.

P. 131.

teeming millions, and pour out my prayers in their behalf. Oh, that this may be a spot blessed by God's presence, and sanctified by the visitations of the Comforter."

CHAPTER X.

Excursions—Tea-Shops — Temple of Tien-Moh-Shan — Budhist Worship—Traveling by Raft—First Sermon in Chinese.

In the spring of 1855 Mr. Aitchison, in company with Rev. Mr. Points, of the American Episcopal Board, made two excursions towards the interior. We give a few incidents of these trips, as recorded in the ever-faithful Journal.

"April 20. At Tsung Zeh we landed and distributed a few books. A crowd soon collecting, we were forced to take refuge in our boats, from which, as we passed along the narrow canal, we handed many volumes to the eager multitude. The news of our arrival spread like wild-fire, and every window and door was full of eyes watching for a glimpse of the strange-looking men. And such eagerness for our books! Oh, that the motive were good! Many actually endangered limb, and even life, in order to become possessors of a volume. May God make the day's work fruitful in good to immortal souls.

"At one place the people seemed to have turned out 'en masse' to get a look at us. The streets were lined with persons eager for a close inspection, while great numbers of women and children filled the doors and windows. What honor! The Emperor himself would not have been received with such demonstrations of—curiosity. Having reached the boat, we were beset with visitors loudly calling for books. To escape their importunity we launched out into the stream, but even then many came to us in boats. Among others two very respectable gentlemen called, wishing for works on medicine.

"April 23. Started early on our return, and retraced our path in the Grand Canal. Next day at noon we reached the walled city Kia-Hing, containing probably about 200,000 inhabitants. We entered the north gate, and emerged from the east gate, followed as usual by a great crowd. The rabble, however, were less noisy and more respectful than at some other times. On returning to the boat, we took some books ashore to distribute. The press was almost intolerable.

Such pushing and snatching I have rarely seen. Men could hardly have displayed more eagerness had every volume been solid gold. Multitudes turned out to see us. The scenes attending the progress of Kossuth through the United States were re-enacted. Such things would be almost insufferable were it not for the thought that every walk of this kind, every exposure to the gaze of the rabble, is a part of the preparation necessary to the success of the Gospel at some future day. The wall of the city seemed to be in excellent order, the streets well paved, and the shops filled with valuable articles.

"April 25. At one village we saw the fishing cormorants. They are large birds looking somewhat like ducks. When not occupied in fishing they roost on sticks projecting over the water from both sides of the boat. When fishing they swim in the water a little in advance of the boat, diving and rising to the surface constantly. I saw one bring up a good-sized fish in his bill. The poor bird tried in vain to swallow his victim, a string round his neck preventing him from accomplishing his purpose. How they are able to hold their struggling, slippery prey is a marvel.

The Fishing Cormorant.

Five Years in China.

P. 134.

"May 16. Had quite a conversation with the boatmen just before dark. Poor fellows! how deep the darkness in which they are groping along their life-path. The contemplation of such individual instances makes me sad. And then to think of these millions! Oh, when shall the glad tidings of mercy reach them all?

"May 18. At Huchau. We arrived here about two o'clock. Had the pleasure of greeting the mountains once more, as they loomed up in the distance. Detained in our boats the whole afternoon by the rain. More serious conversation with the boatmen just before dark. They readily confessed the worthlessness of their gods, and declared them to be of no use. But *ancestral worship* they were not so ready to condemn. This is one of the grand obstacles which the gospel encounters in China. It is a part of the people's life. High and low are equally attached to it. Our reasoning and illustrations seemed to have some effect.

"The poor fellows who work at the oars tell us that their wages are only five hundred cash (about 28 cents) per month. What would American laborers think of such pay? Of course they have their daily rice besides.

"The inhabitants of this region seem to be very poor, but still contented. They often sing while at their work. But oh, how the gospel would elevate them: how it would change the whole aspect of things.

"May 21. Me-chi. Our course to-day has been among the most glorious scenery—mountains on all sides. The land generally lies much higher than at Shanghai. The mulberry-tree is cultivated everywhere. For the last few miles the stream has been filled with rafts of various kinds of wood, particularly bamboo. Hundreds of men are employed in making these, and conveying them to the neighboring cities. The majority of those we saw at work in the fields and on the rafts are very lightly clothed, some of them indeed not clothed at all. A wild song often reached our ears coming from some solitary boatman as he plied his oar.

"As we were approaching a bridge, the old captain came into the cabin and besought us not to speak while passing under it. On asking the reason of the request, he gravely informed us that the genii of the bridge would be grievously offended if a word were uttered. We thought it best not to encourage such a superstitious notion, and therefore continued talking all the time, defying the power of the mysterious spirit, by calling him to come out and injure us. The poor old man seemed quite shocked, but he soon recovered his good humor. This evening he proposes that we keep watch for fear of robbers. In this matter I suspect he is only half in earnest. We only laugh at his fears.

"May 20. We have spent a very quiet Sabbath in this retired place. The rain descended with little intermission till about three o'clock. The state of the paths forbade any attempt at visiting in the neighborhood. Had a little season of pleasant meditation just before dusk. The boatmen hardly understand why we are unwilling to proceed on this day. We overheard the captain telling a visitor that we did not *work*, but only played on the Sabbath. To-morrow we intend to push toward the West. How far we shall advance will depend on circumstances.

"We have been sitting on the bow of our little boat, enjoying the cool breeze and the moonlight.

The natives are busy speculating as to our business in these parts. The conclusion to which most come is that we wish to sell opium, or to buy tea and silk. Whenever it is practicable, we of course correct them, telling our real design, the spreading of Jesus' doctrine, and, secondarily, seeing the country. As I write the wild song alluded to above comes to my ear—how strange my circumstances! Can it be my identical self? the William Aitchison of three years ago?"

At this point the missionaries left their boat, and proceeded on foot over a rugged country, their object being to visit the famous temple of Tien-Moh-Shan, and climb the mountain upon which it stands. Four coolies accompanied them, to carry their books and baggage. "The road," says Mr. Aitchison, "was about two feet wide, paved with flagging stones. Houses and people are few. The ground was swampy, much of the land a mere jungle, not cultivated. Almost every hamlet we passed seemed to be devoted to the raising of silk worms. We saw the cocoons hanging among little bunches of straw, or bamboo wicker-work, prepared for them.

"Every few *li** the road passed through a tea-

* The eighth of a mile.

shop, whose cool benches and refreshing cups invited the weary traveler to a few minutes' rest. In these shops we frequently stopped, while our coolies took a smoke or drank a little tea. We met great numbers of men bringing tea and charcoal from the interior. These generally walked in small companies of eight or ten persons. The sun was oppressively hot; not a cloud, and scarcely a tree to intercept his rays. As we pushed forward briskly, I was soon in a profuse perspiration, so much so that all my clothes were quite saturated.

"About mid-day we reached the walled city Ngan-Kih. Passing straight through it, we halted at the first respectable-*looking* inn of the suburbs. We found very soon that *looks* are deceitful. They furnished us a very poor dinner, and that I tried to eat with chop-sticks. However, we got a little rest and some water in which to bathe our hands and heads. The only way we could keep the rabble from crowding us while eating was by erecting a wooden barricade, a few feet from the table, and defending it vigorously. Thence we proceeded westward a few *li*, when the heat became intolerable. We turned aside therefore to a shady spot, unrolled our bedding, and stretched ourselves out for an hour's repose.

"About four o'clock we again moved, quite refreshed by this brief rest. Just before dark we crossed a stream on a raft, and found ourselves in a small village, where we determined to spend the night. We entered the first inn we came to, and began to examine the accommodations. A single look disgusted us. The only sleeping apartment was a spacious loft, half full of straw, and I suppose quite full of vermin. Mr. Points sallied out to search for a lodging-place, while I attended to the baggage. He soon returned with the news that there was a Budhist temple near by, where we might spend the night. The people here were very rude. We could not get a moment to spend by ourselves. Our supper was set out on the aforesaid loft, and consisted of a few ducks' eggs and a bowl of rice. After this apology for a meal we entered the temple, and ere long were stretched side by side on a table, *trying* to sleep.

"May 23. When we rose from our hard couch it was raining fast, and we began to think of halting for a time. But the shower was only a temporary one, and we were soon on the road. After traveling fifteen *li* we reached the walled city Hian-fong, where we stopped to eat. This place is small, but apparently quite respectable. The streets so far as we saw them, for China, were wide and clean. While in the inn, Mr. Points became quite ill, and I really feared we might be compelled to turn back. After resting, however, for a time on a table, he felt better and we proceeded. Large crowds were waiting in the streets to see us, but not a disrespectful word was uttered in our hearing. Indeed from the hour we left Me-chi, we had not heard the word Pah-kwe-tsz (white devil.)

"May 23. Our route to-day has been through the most magnificent scenery. Mountains, valleys, groves, streams, all in beautiful proportions. The hill-sides were sometimes terraced very neatly, each step up consisting of a fine field of grain. There were no forests, strictly speaking, only small clumps of trees. Some of these trees were the largest I have ever seen. The mountains have a naked appearance, though some of them are covered with bamboo. We frequently crossed the streams on large stones, which, on account of the recent rains, were sometimes several inches under water. The streams were all rapid, and flowed over a rocky bed.

"Saw numerous paper manufactories. The principal machinery consists of an over-shot water-wheel, and an immense trip-hammer which pulverizes the material, (chiefly bamboo), of which the paper is made. At noon we selected a cool, shady place, distant (as we thought) from the haunts of men, where we might rest a while. But before we had fairly spread our mat on the turf, the people were pouring in from all quarters. There was nothing to be gained by feeling provoked, and therefore we tried to keep our temper. But it is really difficult for a man to eat or sleep with an admiring crowd of by-standers eagerly watching every motion he makes, and speculating in no very subdued tones on every article that covers him.

"Before evening Mr. Points felt too tired to proceed on foot, and we therefore called a chair. I resolved to *walk* to the summit of the mountain, and thus do what no foreigner has ever yet done.

"As the shades of evening were gathering around us, we reached a temple, where we stopped for the night. Here we were in no very comfortable place. The priests, to the number of twenty-five, are idle and dirty. They have assigned us a filthy room to sleep in, and we have just been making an unsuccessful attempt to eat some of the dishes set before us. After ten o'clock we heard a terrible thumping of drums and ringing of bells, the signal for evening worship. We looked in, and it was a sad sight. Three boys were left to do the chanting and praying. They stood before the huge idols in the dimly-lighted apartments, and mumbled in a low tone the allotted number of words. Each seemed anxious to outdo the other in the speed of his tongue.

"We said to ourselves, as we looked on, surely this sight is enough to inspire any one with the spirit of missions. What an abomination must such devil-worship be in the view of a holy God. We gave away quite a number of books to-day. These were everywhere eagerly and thankfully received.

"May 24. We started this morning in the rain; were soon pretty thoroughly wet. The scenery became grand in the highest degree. Our course during the whole day has been among the mountains. Much of the time we have been just walking up or down stairs. The road is made principally of large stones, down which the water frequently gushes in small streams. We were often in, and sometimes above the clouds. Now and then as we reached some naked peak and halted a moment for a look, the view was sublime; at our feet was a narrow valley through which a torrent was rushing with a deafening noise, and in the distance mountain piled on mountain as far as the eye could see. One minute it would be clear and bright, the next we were enveloped in vapor. Now there was sunshine, and now rain.

"I had often since coming to China expressed the wish to see a stream of clear water; here to-day I saw scores of them. Some were wide, some narrow: some deep, some shallow: some noisy, some still; all clear as crystal, whether tumbling over the rocks like young Niagaras, or gliding smoothly along over a sandy bottom.

"Before noon I became very tired, and had it not been for my determination to walk, I should have shared the chair with Mr. Points as he begged me to do. Indeed I soon became quite sick.

We halted at noon at a miserable cabin by the road-side where we had expected to find a village. It is called Ta-Ya-Wan, (Great Wild Bend.) The inmates were engaged in pickling the bamboo shoots, of which the children are so fond. While the dinner was preparing, I coiled myself on a bundle of bedding with an umbrella over me, for it began to rain a little, and tried to rest. I made out to swallow a boiled egg, though I felt little appetite."

The next day our missionaries climbed a high mountain, in order to visit the temple at Tien-Moh-Shan, of which the journal gives a minute account. We copy a part.

"The principal priest and his two or three subordinates gave us a hearty welcome, and immediately set before us refreshments, consisting of tea, little cakes, pea-nuts, and a sort of prune. This temple has a splendid location about half way up the mountain. It is surrounded by numerous pines of a giant growth. Many of them have a girth of fifteen feet. The murmur of falling water is heard day and night. From various points you get a view of the valley below, while above the mountain rises in its grandeur. We were, however, too weary to enjoy or examine the scenery this evening.

"Just after dark, worship was performed in the room adjoining ours, by one solitary priest. The apartment was dimly lighted by two candles, burning on the altar before the principal idol, Budh. Incense sticks were smoking before other inferior gods. There was something really solemn in the service. The officiating priest in a plaintive, wailing tone, recited the prayers, every now and then striking a deep sounding bell or a hollow piece of wood. Doubtless the circumstances, including the deep gloom of the landscape without, had much to do with my feelings. Oh, how I rejoiced that I knew the living God and Jesus Christ, his Son!

"May 20. Had a good rest last night; Mr. Points on a table, and I on a settee. Immediately after breakfast, we set out for the summit of the mountain, which is said to be about ten *li* from this temple. The path was steep and rugged, in many places over-grown with shrubs and briars. We were exactly an hour in making the ascent. The view surpassed all that we had previously seen. As far as vision extended in all directions were mountains. The intervening valleys were cultivated, many of them ornamented with a streamlet which shone like a thread of silver. The objects of interest on the summit are a small natural bridge of rock, under which some Chinese characters are carved in stone, and a grotto, at the entrance of which is a fine spring of water.

"Most of the afternoon has been spent in writing. After tea we walked down the mountain path a short distance, enjoying the moonlight. Here we united in singing, 'When I can read my title clear'—'All hail the power of Jesus' name,' and 'There is a land of pure delight.' For the first time, I presume, these solitudes echoed the praises of Jehovah. Oh, may the time soon come when all who resort hither shall make the beautiful groves around this temple vocal with hymns of praise.

"These priests of Budha remind one very much of the descriptions of the 'jolly friars' of the middle ages. Some of them are intelligent, many are as stupid as a man can well be.

"Thoughts of home, (where is it ?) and of dear ones whom I shall never again see on earth, come over me to-night. God bless all whom I love, now and evermore!

"May 26. As soon as breakfast was finished, we set out to visit the temple at the foot of the mountain. Our host, the old priest, led the way, habited according to my idea of a pilgrim in the time of the crusades. He wore a broad-brimmed article, which answered the double purpose of a hat and a sun-shade. In his hand he carried a long mountain staff. We followed, dressed in white for the most part, accompanied by three coolies, one of whom had a bundle of books slung over his shoulder. The path was really a staircase, winding among groves and precipices. A pine tree, which we took the trouble to measure, had a circumference of twenty-four feet seven inches. There were many of nearly the same size, though this seemed to be the acknowledged patriarch of the region.

"A number of hermitages perched in the wildest places seemed to invite the weary traveler to frequent rests. These were generally occupied by single priests who were in solitude trying to merit the heaven of their sect. One of these abodes was half the work of man, and half of nature. Within a dark chamber whose roof appeared to be the solid rock, was a huge structure of plaster before which worship was paid by the devout visitor.

"After a wearisome descent we reached the temple, and it is truly a magnificent structure. Like all the Chinese buildings, it covers much space, without being very high. One would need a guide if he wished to make a thorough and satisfactory survey of all its parts. From the main entrance there is a gradual ascent by paved walks through spacious courts, till you reach the hall in which the gods and their worshipers reside. There are, as we were informed, upwards of two hundred priests and a hundred laymen attached to the establishment. In certain months, and on the recurrence of certain festivals, multitudes resort thither from the adjoining provinces.

"We were at once introduced to the head priest in his own rooms. He is a tall, spare man with a gentle manner and not unpleasing expression. He was dressed in a yellow robe, and wore shoes of the same color. Tea and sweet-meats were immediately set before us.

Others crowded into the room, but still paid considerable deference to their superior. After a few minutes' conversation, we proceeded to inspect the premises. The arrangements for feeding such a number of persons, were well worth seeing, the kitchens and dining-room being very large. The priests were exceedingly polite and hospitable. Many of them had their beads in hand, counting their prayers after the manner of the Romanists. There were some interesting and attractive faces. How sad the sight of so many poor wretches, thus blindly groping after heaven.

"We left upward of a hundred volumes among them, all of which were thankfully received. On leaving, many followed us to the outer gate, seeming loth to have us depart. It is not strange that they take pleasure in anything that breaks the dull monotony of their life.

"Immediately after parting with them I broke Mr. Points' cane in the vain attempt to break a large serpent's back. Snakes, lizards and centipedes abound, judging from the number I have already seen. The returning walk was exceedingly wearisome, and I truly rejoice in the prospect of to-morrow's rest. Would that I had the prospect of entering some church to worship God with the great congregation.

"May 27. Sabbath. A day of rest indeed. Called upon a priest who lives in the wildest spot we have yet seen, about a quarter of a mile from the temple. He is the most interesting man we have met on the mountain. His hermitage is reached by a descending staircase, where a false step would be destruction. The life of such a Budhist must be very like that of the monks of the early ages. The voluntary offerings of those who resort hither for worship constitute his only means of subsistence, unless perchance he cultivates a piece of ground, or engages in some other branch of manual labor. Most of them seem contented with their lot.

"May 28. Rose at four, and in less than an hour we were on the road, bound for Shanghai. The morning among the mountains was most glorious. The sun rose in his strength, and the deep shadows fled from their hiding-places at his approach. The air was pure and bracing, and all of us were in high spirits. The road which had been so weary for days before, was now delightful. At eight o'clock we reached Ta-Ya-Wan, and by noon we were in Tsung-Tsong, having walked about fifty *li*. A raft was immediately engaged, or rather a pair of them. Two men besides ourselves and our baggage were to be taken to Me-chi for one dollar and four hundred cash. While we were eating dinner at the inn of the village, the rafts were got ready, and we at once embarked amid a crowd of wondering spectators. We were highly pleased with this, to us, novel mode of traveling. The river was full of rapids, down which we glided with amazing velocity and yet perfect safety. Two men managed each raft. In the course of two hours we reached a small hamlet, where our raftsmen resided. A room was prepared for our accommodation, which, though the best in the house, was disgustingly filthy. During the night Mr. Points and myself occupied a chair and a narrow bench alternately. Of course we slept almost none at all.

"May 29. We were stirring early, but not so the raftsmen. A man needs a vast amount of patience to travel in China, especially if he is in haste. At last, the due number of bowls of rice being despatched by our Chinese hands, we got started."

The party returned to Shanghai on the 4th of June, in which city Mr. Aitchison passed the remainder of the summer. Two brief entries in his journal mark an important epoch in his missionary life.

"September 1. This day completed my first year in Shanghai. Truly goodness and mercy have followed me every step of my way. Seldom have I enjoyed better health during a period equally long. It has been emphatically a year of *preparation.* I have attempted little in the way of direct effort for the salvation of those around me. May all the attainments of the year be consecrated to my Redeemer, and may the future, be it long or short, bear witness to the sincerity of my love for Christ and souls.

"Sept. 2. To-day, which is Sabbath, I preached my first sermon in Chinese. My audience consisted of Mrs. Bridgman's school and a few others. My text was in Matt. vi. 9, 10. I occupied about ten minutes' time. Though the effort was painful, it was very pleasant. How blessed the privilege of thus preaching Christ among the heathen, though it may be with a stammering tongue. Two persons were baptized by Dr. Bridgman, one of them a pupil, and the other an elderly woman who resides in the city. The Lord grant them a large measure of his grace."

THE PUNISHMENT OF A CHINESE THIEF.

CHAPTER XI.

Friendship with Rev. J. S. Burdon—Change of Plan—Boat Life —Soong-Kiang—Worship of Confucius—Mohammedans.

DURING the year thus propitiously closed, Mr. Aitchison formed the acquaintance of Rev. John S. Burdon, of the English Church Missionary Society. The following letter to Rev. Dr. Anderson gives some account of the peculiar and delightful attachment which sprang up between them, and of an entire change of plan for missionary labor adopted by these brethren in concert.

"SOONG-KIANG, *Feb.* 1, 1856.

"REV. AND DEAR SIR:—Believing that you would be glad to have a more particular account of myself than is contained in the Mission Letter, I send you some details of my present mode of life. My acquaintance with the Rev. Mr. Burdon, the companion of all my wanderings and labors, commenced in the early part of last summer. He had been severely afflicted by the death, first of his wife, and then of his only child. Fellowship in grief soon drew our hearts closely together. It was not long before each found in the other a similarity of views and purposes in regard to the prosecution of the missionary work in China. We longed to come into more immediate contact with the people, degraded and prejudiced though they are. We longed to pass the barriers which the exclusive policy of the Chinese, and the mistaken policy of foreign treaty-makers, had combined to erect in the path of Christianity. We longed to carry the glad tidings of salvation to the millions around Shanghai, who are reached only during occasional flying visits of the missionary.

"Our first step was to hire a house within the walls of the city from which we could make excursions into the surrounding country at our pleasure. There we resided for three months, devoting ourselves to hard study, and maturing our plans for the future. We concluded, however, to abandon our house, which we had only designed to make the headquarters of our operations, and to give ourselves wholly to the business of itinerating. On the 30th of October last we started on our first trip; and from that date the boat has been our constant home, although the period for which we had rented our house did not expire until the 24th of December.

"I trust you will agree with me in thinking our course a wise one, in the circumstances. Shanghai enjoys the labors of more than twenty ordained missionaries; while this immense plain, teeming with immortal souls, is left for the most part unoccupied, except by the never-tiring and well nigh omnipresent emissaries of Rome. More than a dozen walled cities, besides almost innumerable towns and villages, are embraced within the limits of our parish.

"It is our design to spend at one place from a week to a month, or even longer, according to its importance, or the encouragement we meet with, returning to it again in regular order, when our circuit shall have been completed. The city from which I write, Sung-kiang, lies to the south-west of Shanghai, distant twenty-five or thirty miles. Its population is probably equal to that of Boston. We have been here already nearly three weeks.

"The accommodations of our boat are not particularly spacious. A cabin, nine feet by seven, answers the purposes of parlor, dining-room and bed-chamber for both of us. A Chinese teacher, servant, and four boatmen, complete our party. Where they all stow themselves at night, is still a mystery to me. Our forenoons are spent in study, our afternoons in preaching and conversing with the people.

"I wish you could accompany us to the front of some temple, where we usually address the crowd. As we approach the spot, noisy boys rush before us, like so many heralds, sometimes shouting at the top of their voices, 'The barbarians are come,' or 'Ya-Soo, Ya-Soo!' (Jesus, Jesus.) By the time we get to our pulpit, usually a stone step, or other convenient elevation, we are hemmed in on all sides by the eager rabble. At once we commence discoursing on the grand theme of redemption. With the open heaven, where reigns the only true God, above us; with the hideous images of a corrupt and corrupting heathenism around us, and a multitude of immortal but perishing men before us, you will not wonder that we sometimes feel the stirrings of an unwonted inspiration.

"The fear of giving offence rarely modifies a phrase of our address. The pleasure of the auditors appears to be commensurate with the amount of ridicule heaped upon the senseless objects of their worship. The majority pay respectful attention. Such a motley collection, however, is almost sure to contain some 'rowdies,' who busy themselves with absurd speculations about our clothes or our persons. Occasionally a nut-shell, or something equally harmless, is tossed at us from behind by some fellow of the baser sort. The sermon or rather 'talk' being ended, we give an opportunity to any one to ask questions. Too often ignorance prompts some frivolous inquiry, and thus diverts the mind from more serious matters. At times, considerable useful discussion is thus elicited. Opium and the papists, equally the curse of the empire, are the most frequent topics of interrogation; and they are destined to be, as I think, the mightiest obstacles to the triumph of vital religion. A number of persons always follow us to our boat, to whom we give books, if they can read.

"Towards evening, commonly, we have calls from respectable people, most of whom come ostensibly to learn our doctrine, but really to gratify their curiosity. We invariably make Christianity the principal theme of our conversation, bringing our visitors back to it as often as they wander, which is not seldom. We have thus far met with little open opposition in our work. Ill-bred lads are our greatest annoyance. They follow us everywhere, racing and shouting at our heels, as though we were wild animals, or something worse. Once stones were thrown at us by some mischievous person in a crowd. None of these things move us. We have entered upon these labors at the call of God; and we will not fear what man can do unto us. Amid discouragements of every sort, we comfort ourselves with the hope that the Lord is sending us 'before his face, into every city and place whither he himself would come.' What an honor, if we may be employed in preparing the way before him! A glorious mission field will this be, when the day of his merciful visitation shall have come! The seed now cast into the hard soil by the weary laborer, will then spring up and bear fruit unto life eternal. Even if ours be only the task of breaking up the fallow ground, we will yet rejoice in this as the appointed antecedent of the wished-for harvest."

Speaking of these labors in another place, he says:—"It often happens that some one asks for medicine to cure him of a habit of smoking opium. Our usual reply is that a firm determination is the best medicine. One asks if we abstain from animal food, like the Budhist priests. We reply that these things are not important. Another asks if we are the same as Roman Catholics. We tell him, no; and perhaps add a word of explanation."

Again he writes, "I wish you could hear and understand some of my conversations with my teacher. He is a decided Confucianist, or more properly infidel. He is never weary of raising objections to the system of Christian doctrine contained in the Bible. According to him, our religion is the same as that of the Budhists. Alike we pray morning and evening, say grace before meals, reverence our sacred books, and expect future retribution. He never takes the trouble to penetrate beneath the surface of things;

never investigates the evidences by which the opposing claims are supported. Closing his eyes, he denies the existence of the sun, and rushes blindly upon an unknown, mysterious destiny. He professes to believe in the transmigration of souls, but I greatly doubt his sincerity. He may be taken as a fair representative of the reading men of China. Were he truly converted, Christianity would find in him an able champion. My heart's desire and prayer to God is, that he may soon become the subject of renewing grace, and thus be fitted to preach the gospel to his benighted countrymen."

In another place Mr. Aitchison says:—"Daily we have plenty of visitors, but, alas! not one whose heart seems touched by the Holy Spirit. They come to see and be seen; and sooner or later some sinister motive becomes apparent in those individuals we had thought most hopeful. There is an idea universally prevalent among them that connection with foreigners will better their worldly circumstances; and this is the secret spring of many a question which seems sincere. Distrust is the prominent feeling in our minds, even when conversing with those who are apparently serious.

"It is hard to labor among and in behalf of a people who despise you. It is hard to be called an ignorant barbarian by a man who does not know that the earth is round. It is hard to be followed through the streets by noisy boys, shouting all sorts of insults, and occasionally throwing small stones at your head. It is hard to be considered an opium seller, disguising an iniquitous trade by fair discourses on virtue. It is hard to practise self-denial for the benefit of those who would rejoice in your misfortune. And yet such hardness must the good soldier of Jesus Christ endure in this empire. It is glorious, however, to be brought into such fellowship with the Redeemer. It is glorious to feel that his presence abides with us. It is glorious to know that if we suffer for him, we shall also reign with him. Then welcome every reproach, every privation, every form of trial! Welcome even death itself, if it be for his name!"

The journal adds some matters of peculiar interest respecting the country.

"21. Our forenoon walk brought us to the

temple of Kwanti, the famous demi-god of China. Everything seemed to be in good order, and this can be said of few temples, at least in this region. In front of the principal image was a tablet containing the words, 'Emperor, ten thousand years, ten thousand years, ten thousand times ten thousand years!' This tablet and inscription are a common thing in front of images. The design seems to be that the worshiper of the idol may by the same act pay homage to the sovereign.

"After the usual preaching this afternoon, a young man came to the boat ostensibly to inquire about this new doctrine. He seemed quite intelligent and sincere. This evening he came again, bringing with him two companions. We had a long conversation on various subjects, religion being of course the prominent one. Allusion was made by them to the holy water of the Romanists, and to the worship of the cross. After their departure, the boatman informed us that he heard them just before reaching the boat say to each other, 'We care nothing for these doctrines, but let us enter and inquire how we may rid ourselves of opium-smoking habits.' It was rather discouraging to know that this was the secret of

Chinese temple worship.

Five Years in China. P. 164.

all their apparent interest in Christianity. It is shocking to think of the extent to which the use of opium is carried. It came out in the course of the evening's interview that it was common for gentlemen to have a guest-chamber fitted up with all the apparatus for inhaling the poisonous drug.* This single cause threatens to destroy this entire nation. Surely God will arrest in some way the flowing tide of evil; how He alone knows. Man can scarcely form a conjecture.

"22. This morning, when returning from our usual walk, we met quite a cavalcade of mandarins and their attendants, some in sedans, some on horseback, some on foot. On inquiring the cause of the procession, we were informed that they were proceeding to the Kwan-ti temple to give thanks in behalf of the Emperor for a new mother, who had been adopted to fill the place of his own, recently deceased. Curiosity prompted us to follow them. Reaching the temple we were immediately surrounded by the crowd, who asked

* The habit of smoking opium is rapidly increasing. It is now estimated that hundreds of thousands die annually in consequence of this degrading practice. While the rich man has a room in his own house fitted up for the purpose, the poor resorts to some public place, or the opium-smoker's den, for his indulgence.

all sorts of questions about our clothes, &c. Fortunately for us the ceremony soon commenced. The mandarins, to the number of fifteen or twenty, dressed in rich fur robes, arranged themselves in two rows in front of the temple. Some were military gentlemen, and some civil. Soon there was a flourish of trumpets, and a yellow sedan was observed approaching, borne on the shoulders of a dozen or more men. Down went the two rows of dignitaries on their knees, while the chair, carrying the Imperial Message, passed between into the temple court. In an instant all were again on their feet, and following the chair. Before half of them had entered the door, the rabble made a push forward, and soon their highnesses were jammed among the elbowing ragamuffins. There seemed to be little respect felt, as there was certainly little shown, for the powers that be. Waiting till the rush was over, we went in, and found all the *buttoned* personages kneeling before the image. Soon the mandarin who presides over the reading community reverently took the Imperial document in his hands, and mounting a stage, prepared to read it. First, however, there was a series of genuflexions and 'knocking heads.' One old man standing on an elevated step would shout, 'Kneel!' and down all would fall on their knees; 'Worship!' and every head bowed to the earth; 'Rise!' and all were on their feet. This and the reading being ended, the mandarins betook themselves to an inner temple, where we were not allowed to follow them.

"This afternoon we both preached in our usual places. After the sermons, two young men came to visit us. They made many intelligent inquiries, showing that they had already acquired a considerable knowledge of the facts of Christianity. Their ideas were rather *Romanistic*.

"23. This morning visited the Confucian temple. Its interior is very similar to that in other places. There are the same inscriptions in praise of the Sage, and the same tablets to the Master and his principal disciples. The following is the inscription on the tablet of Confucius: 'The most holy teacher Confucius' spiritual tablet.' It is somewhat of a relief in China to stand in a temple where no grinning deformity called 'god' stared at me from his dusty shrine. And this is generally the case in Confucian temples.

preaching we were quite thronged with visitors. The principal topic of conversation was Christ and him crucified.

"24. Before leaving our boat for the temple, two young men called. All their inquiries had reference to the difference between our doctrines and those of the Papists. They seemed to be pretty well acquainted with the chief errors of Rome. We cannot avoid a feeling of regret, that regard for the truth compels us to disown those who are professedly engaged in the same work with ourselves. We learned that in this city there is a chapel surmounted by a cross. Disciples are now made openly. Were we willing to baptize men on the same conditions as they, we might count our converts by the hundreds. Baptized heathenism is, however, little if any better than mere heathenism.

"After preaching we had visitors until sunset. We tried to be faithful to the souls of all. Just before nine o'clock this evening, my name was called from the shore, and on my replying, three young men came on board. We immediately invited them to enter our little cabin, and had considerable discourse with them. What possible object they could have I know not, unless Nicodemus-like they came under cover of night to inquire the way of salvation. Inasmuch as we have to deal with a crafty people, we build no hopes on such circumstances. Their real purpose may be disclosed on a second visit. The number of those who have come to us in a few days, encourages us to pray with renewed earnestness, that the Lord would make us a blessing to these multitudes. With him is the residue of the Spirit. When he speaks the word, there will *be light* among this people.

"25. One of our visitors of last night came again to-day, and after some introductory conversation, his real object was disclosed. He wished to sell us a quantity of timber which he had on hand! The people seem to think that a foreigner is made of gold. Such discoveries of insincerity and selfishness on the part of some render us suspicious of all.

"27. Sabbath. This forenoon we took our station in one of the temples of the western suburb. A few gathered around us, with whom we soon entered into conversation on the all-important subject of the soul. While alluding incidentally to the evil of opium smoking, we were violently assaulted by a man charging upon us foreigners all the curse which the drug entails. He inveighed against us some time in a towering passion, the burden of his speech being that it was impossible that the doctrine of the West could be good. A few words of explanation dispelled some of his false notions and mollified his rage. To the last, however, he persisted in ascribing to the barbarians the miseries of his countrymen. Oh! this awful curse! When and how is it to be removed? Would that all who have a hand in introducing this poison could have listened to his truly eloquent denunciation of their iniquitous traffic.

"In the afternoon we preached as usual, first within, and then outside the city. On returning we were followed by a respectably-dressed young man, who soon introduced himself as desirous of forming our acquaintance. We invited him to our boat, when we had a long conversation on the subject of Budhism. He insisted that the priests of China preached the same doctrine with us, though they used a different phraseology. To the best of our ability we pointed out several important differences, admitting at the same time that the system of Budhism had in it a grain of truth. He wrote out for us a quotation from one of their classics, which undeniably and yet vaguely pointed to one, self-existent Being, who was the author of all created existences. The young man seems to be one of that rare class in China, who possess naturally a religious turn of mind. He seems to be groping after the true way. After the experience of the past week, of course, we are not sanguine, but we hope for the best.

"28. After a little excursion to one of the neighboring hills, in the course of which we fell in with our fellow-itinerants, Messrs. Burns and Taylor, on their way to Soong-Kiang, we returned to our boats about four o'clock. No sooner had we entered it than an elderly gentleman appeared, and pulling from some recess in his ample garments a tract, politely begged for more particular instruction in regard to the doctrines it contained. Its subject was the Death of Altamont. I did not learn how long it had been in his possession. We briefly explained to him the important steps involved in becoming a

Christian. As he told us he was going to Shanghai we directed him to Dr. Bridgman, as a teacher who would be happy to guide him in the path of knowledge. The old gentleman left us with many professions of gratitude for our kindness. May the Lord lead him to the Lamb of God that taketh away the sin of the world.

"Feb. 2. Nothing new in the mode or the result of our labors. Numbers of people call upon us, but none manifest particular evidence of the Spirit's work.

"Feb. 3. Sabbath. According to previous appointment, Messrs. Burns and Taylor came to our boat, where we together celebrated the dying love of Christ in partaking of the communion. For many reasons the occasion will long be remembered with interest. We sat together in heavenly places. We four represented as many denominations of Christians,—Episcopalian, Presbyterian, Baptist, Congregationalist. Mr. Burns officiated. It was the first time in his life, though he had been in the ministry seventeen years. He read and commented on the fifth chapter of Revelation. Afterwards he made some interesting remarks appropriate to the occasion. All of us in succession offered prayer. It was, I think, the most profitable communion season I ever enjoyed.

"Feb. 4. Long before daylight we were on the way to Shanghai. The wind soon rose and we were unable to proceed. Our little boat was tossed like an egg-shell on the river. After the wind moderated a little we again got under way. About half-past six o'clock we anchored at Shanghai."

The summer of 1856 was spent in Shanghai, "as it would have been fool-hardy," Mr. Aitchison writes, "to brave the fierce sun of this climate. As soon as the cool weather came on," he adds, "I took to the boat again, in company with my beloved Brother Burdon. He is a true yoke-fellow in the Lord. His society has been a rich boon to me. We sympathize perfectly on all subjects but that of church government, and there we agree to differ."

August 10th he wrote, "We were quite interested last week in three Mohammedans who introduced themselves to us. One was from Nanking, one from Hangchau, and one from Suchau. It was refreshing to hear them affirm that they worshiped the 'one true God.' They seemed to know little more of the peculiar sect to which they belong than the name of its founder, the impostor of Mecca. According to their account, there are vast numbers of Mohammedans scattered through the empire. They worship God five times a day, turning their faces toward the west. Strangely enough they profess their belief in Jesus as a Saviour, drawing some distinction between him and the false prophet which I could not fully understand. Such men as they seem not far from the kingdom of God.

"It is known also for a certainty that there is a community of Jews in the interior, who have manuscript portions of the Old Testament in the original Hebrew. Such things are a pleasing testimony to the truth of some parts of biblical and even profane history.

CHAPTER XII.

Ping-Hoo—Reasons for being there—Cheerless Abode—Joy in God—Importance of the Step—Darkness of Heathenism.

THUS Mr. Aitchison passed the second year of his missionary life, "not slothful in business, fervent in spirit, serving the Lord." But he and Mr. Burdon had felt for some time, that, although their boat-life had some advantages, yet it lacked that permanency and concentration of effort necessary to the most enduring results; and they began to cast about for some place where they might settle down, at least for a time, and try what might be done by another mode of operation. The following letter to Rev. Dr. Anderson contains a deeply interesting account of their attempt to establish themselves in a large town, at a considerable distance from the coast.

PING-HOO, *Dec.* 31, 1856.

"REV. AND DEAR SIR:—You will begin to think that my correspondence with the Board is likely to take the shape of an annual letter. For myself I can scarcely believe that a whole year has passed since my last communication. True indeed is the Chinese proverb, 'Time is like an arrow—days and months are like a weaver's shuttle.' When I become better acquainted with this most difficult of all languages, and am able to give more of my strength to the direct preaching of the gospel, I hope to write more frequently.

"So far as my missionary life is concerned, the last twelve months may be divided into three periods. Up to the early part of July, I continued my labors as an itinerant, sometimes penetrating to a considerable distance into the interior. The three hottest months of summer were spent in Shanghai, Rev. Mr. Burdon and myself taking our meals and studying together in the city, but sleeping at the houses of friends outside the walls. Early in October we took to our boats again, with the intention, however, of doing our best to secure a permanent footing in some place more or less remote from the influence of the foreign community. Through the blessing of God this intention has been carried into effect, and we now occupy our own hired house in the city whose name heads this sheet.

"Ping-Hoo is situated in the northern part of Chekiang Province, about seventy miles from Shanghai. Its population, including the suburbs, we estimate at nearly 100,000. It stands in the midst of a vast plain, thoroughly cultivated and densely populated. One solitary mountain is visible in the Southern horizon, a peak of the range which forms the barrier of Hangchau Bay. Were the entire country open to us, we would by no means select this as the most promising place for a missionary station. But in present circumstances we must do as we can, not as we would. While the people remain as prejudiced and proud as they now are, while jealous authorities watch with a suspicious eye every movement of the foreign barbarians, and while human treaties exclude us from the perishing millions of the vast interior, we gladly take possession, in Christ's name, of any spot outside the 'five ports.'

"But I must tell you how we came here and what we are doing. Feeling the importance of permanency and concentration, we have from the first cherished the hope of establishing the centre of our operations at some distance from Shanghai. That port is, in our opinion, a most unpromising field for missionary effort. Whether it be owing to the fact that the practice of the many among foreigners gives the lie to the teaching of the few, or to some other cause, it is undeniable that the gospel seems greatly hindered there. Few of the natives profess to believe its doctrines, and those few seem sadly wanting in the graces necessary to adorn their profession. It has seemed at least possible to us, that elsewhere the obstacles might be fewer and the progress of the truth more rapid. At any rate it is time to try more aggressive measures than have been hitherto thought expedient. As I survey the moral wastes of this great empire, the question often suggests itself, what would Paul do, were he landed at one of these ports, with the broad commission in his hand, 'Go ye into all the world, and preach the gospel to every creature?' Would he be content to abide by the consular regulations, and revolve in the narrow circle which they define? Would it be long before the gospel was proclaimed in all the chief cities, even in the imperial capital itself?

"With a view to such a permanent settlement as was hinted at above, we sent a catechist of the Church Missionary Society to this place, some time in August last. He secured a small room in the suburbs, and immediately sent us notice of the fact. About the middle of September Mr. Burdon followed him, and with the landlord's consent, crept by night into an upper room of the same house. Three weeks passed quietly, although the authorities were doubtless cognizant of all that transpired. Early in October I arrived, and, after protracted negotiations, we entered into an agreement with the landlord to the following effect. We were to leave the place for three weeks, on a long purposed visit to Ningpo, the port next south of us. During our absence the house was to be vacated by its present occupants and everything made ready for our reception. Seven dollars were to be paid at once as earnest-money, and seven more on our return; these fourteen dollars to be the rent of the premises for the first six months. We paid the seven dollars as stipulated, and took our departure for Ningpo, October 20. In reference to that visit, of which we retain a most delightful remembrance, I will say nothing here, except that our spirits were refreshed by communion with our fellow-missionaries of various denominations, and our faith strengthened by witnessing proofs of God's converting presence even in China.

"On the 15th of November we returned, and anchoring our boat in a retired place, sent for the catechist who had been left in charge. In answer to our inquiries as to the state of things, he informed us that various objections were made by a person who claimed to be the real owner of the house. Suspecting that the whole affair was only a plan to squeeze more money out of us, we paid little attention to the representations made. That night, under cover of the darkness, we transferred ourselves, with bed and baggage, to the upper story of our new abode. Everything was done as privately as possible, with a view to escape the notice of the rabble.

"A few words will serve to describe the residence we were so overjoyed to get possession of. Its two habitable rooms are separated by a wooden partition, the door between them being made by the removal of one wide board. They were both cold, dark and dirty. Not a gleam of sunshine entered the one that fell to my lot. One inner wall was so much out of the perpendicular, that the area beneath it was forbidden ground to all our household. And yet this miserable apology for a house we were not permitted to retain without a continual struggle. Absurd reports were spread among the neighbors, and the landlord became, or at least professed to be, afraid of a disturbance. On the 8th of December he gave us notice to leave the premises at the end of the month. With heavy hearts we meditated on the probability that our enterprise was thus to end, and prayed that God would interpose in our behalf. Our assistant was directed to seek another house, and as the month drew near its close one was offered us. We accepted the proposed terms without hesitation, and on last Saturday, December 27, effected our removal. Our present abode is an improvement on the last, but is like all Chinese dwellings, exceedingly uncomfortable. Friends would smile to see our bare and cheerless rooms, but we would not exchange them for a palace. We are not without the presence of God, and that makes up for the loss of all earthly comforts."

In another letter Mr. Aitchison says, "My furniture consists of a bed, a chair, a small table, a bench, and a trunk, while the naked tiles above are the only roof; and yet I would not exchange this humble hovel for a king's palace. God is here to bless and to give peace. We are laboring to advance his cause, and he will not leave his servants to toil alone. The shadows of great afflictions sometimes indeed darken our path; we sigh over vanished joys, and are ready to faint under the burden of our griefs; but faith points onward, and we press with more eager footsteps to the goal."

"Having thus told you how we came here, I proceed to give you an idea of what we are doing. At first we kept very quietly within doors, not deeming it expedient to show ourselves, much less to preach in the public streets. The report of our arrival soon spread everywhere, and we thought it well to let the people become accustomed to the idea before they actually felt the reality of our presence. This secret policy is quite abhorrent to the spirit of Protestant missions, and we gladly discarded it as soon as the way seemed prepared for the more open propagation of the truth. For upwards of three weeks past, we have gone almost daily into the city and delivered our message in the most crowded thoroughfares. Our audiences listen with much apparent interest, and the intellectual knowledge of Christianity is plainly on the increase. The number who come for private conversation is also much larger than at the outset. In a few cases we have almost hoped that the Holy Spirit was commencing his awakening work on the heart, but as yet we can speak confidently of none. A few books have been distributed among those who seemed able to appreciate their contents. For myself, I think the importance of that branch of missionary effort in China has been somewhat overrated. The number of intelligent readers is much fewer than most persons unacquainted with the facts would suppose. We have been somewhat inclined to open a school, but have as yet come to no decision on the subject.

"The gross darkness in which the heathen mind is enveloped is strikingly exhibited in the inquiries sometimes proposed or remarks made. Error in China is stereotyped, and on that account difficult of correction. You may repeat over and over again the truth, God alone is to be worshiped, explaining to them his perfections and attributes; then ask your hearers what is the proper object of worship, and the answer will be in nine cases out of ten, 'Heaven and earth.' Make the necessary correction, and reason at length on the absurdity of paying homage to the lifeless creature instead of the living Creator, then repeat your question, and the reply will be in many cases as before, 'Heaven and earth,' or possibly modified by the omission of earth.

"Preach to them Christ and him crucified, relate the story of his birth, his instructions, his miracles, his death; show the need of an atonement for sin, and the way in which the Son of God provided it; and when you have finished the discourse, some one will inquire if Christ is the King of England. Talk of the soul, its nature and destiny, the bliss or woe that await it, the wisdom of lightly esteeming this world, and of seeking heaven's happiness, and not unlikely some apparently serious auditor will interrupt you by begging to know the price of your coat.

"We find, notwithstanding, considerable satisfaction in our labors. This city and its neighborhood are regarded as our parish. Acquaintances are beginning to be formed. Prejudice is wearing away. The report of our doctrines and object is spreading in all directions. We see the first faint glimmer of that light which is destined to increase more and more unto the perfect day. May it not be that the Lord has chosen us to be the dispensers of his grace to some of these benighted souls? We are not without the hope that our residence here, unimportant as it may seem to some, will be followed by a blessing whose consequences will extend beyond the immediate circle of our operations.

"In regard to our future prospects, I cannot speak confidently. Our stay here depends upon the will of the authorities, or the disposition of the people, both rather capricious. We know not what a day may bring forth. The present calm may be but the precursor of the coming storm. It would be strange if, in the face of the treaty, we should be permitted to remain for any length of time. There is another contingency worthy of mention. Affairs at Canton wear a threatening aspect. Americans and English seem equally involved in the yet unfinished struggle. Should the war now local become general, there will be no safety for foreigners beyond the reach of their men-of-war guns. Taking all things into consideration, I am not very sanguine as to the permanency of our abode here. The next mail may carry with it the news of our return to Shanghai, or at least our departure from Ping-Hoo. We will strive to work while, in a double sense, the day lasts.

"Is it not time that China was occupying a more prominent place in the missionary work? How vast the population, how urgent their necessities, how few the laborers! The commotions at Canton and at Nanking will doubtless result in increased facilities for prosecuting the work of evangelization; perhaps in the overthrow of those barriers which ages of prejudice have reared and fortified. Where are the youthful soldiers of the cross who are prepared to enter in and possess the land? Come over and help us! There is room for hundreds of apostolic laborers."

In another letter Mr. Aitchison says of his residence at Ping-Hoo:—"The step is one of some importance, as may be seen by a reference to the past. No Protestant missionary ever resided so far from the five ports for so long a time; nor has any Romanist done so, I imagine, in his own European costume. We cannot but hope that a precedent is established which will hasten the day of China's redemption. Freedom to penetrate the interior, and reside where we please, would be a great advance on anything that has yet happened. This city is not very pleasantly situated; nor are its inhabitants prepossessing. Could we choose our place of labor, we should go elsewhere; but for the present we must be content with what we can get."

CHAPTER XIII.

Still at Ping-Hoo—Burdon returns to Shanghai—Interesting Cases—China opening—To Ningpo—Mr. Burdon's Wedding—Remarkable Cascade.

ON the 31st of March, 1857, Mr. Aitchison wrote:* "I regret to say that about the first of February circumstances compelled my dear brother Burdon to return to Shanghai, and there take up his abode. His only colleague in the mission was compelled by ill health to sail for England, leaving a large house and boarding-school without an occupant and superintendent. The path of duty was thus plainly marked out for him, and we were compelled to dissolve our agreeable copartnership. Our experience demonstrated, to ourselves at least, the practicability of union among Christians of various denominations. Each retained his own opinions on questions of doctrine and ecclesiastical government,

* To the Mission House.

and at the same time respected the opinions of the other. Common interests, labors, and hopes bound us together, and kept our hearts in harmony. Oh for the realization of a like union among all the members of the Church of Christ!

"I was not left long alone. Mr. Blodget visited me early in February, and soon after his departure I was joined by Rev. Mr. Edkins, of the London Missionary Society, the companion, as you will remember, of my first excursion into the interior. We shall continue to labor together, at least until the way is open to the 'regions beyond.' Mr. Macy is entertaining the question of a removal northward on account of the commotions at Canton. If he comes I shall hope to have his company in the delightful privations and labors of the itinerant life."

In regard to their services in Ping-Hoo, Mr. Aitchison adds:—

"Some of the neighbors have already formed the *habit* of coming to listen. A few occasionally remain to attend family worship. I wish you could be present at one of these social exercises. As we all, preacher, teacher, and servants read the Bible in turn, verse by verse, you would be struck with the difference of the various dialects. Our household, including boatmen, comprise individuals from various parts of the Empire. There is one from Peking, one from Shantung, one from Nanking, one from Hoo-chow, one from Noo-sih, and one from Shanghai. All these differ considerably in the pronunciation and arrangement of words. We thus exhibit the spectacle, on a small scale, of a second Babel, or as I would prefer to say, a second Pentecost. Oh that each one of the number was intent on declaring the wonderful works of God!

"After a brief exposition and application of the portion of Scripture read, we sing a hymn and unite in prayer, in which latter exercise all reverently kneel, whatever may be the real state of their hearts. These seasons are pleasant and profitable. The Chinese see that our devotions are rational and heartfelt, very different from the mummeries practiced in their temples and dwellings.

"As yet I have little to report in the way of visible success. Some cases, however, have awakened hope in my breast, and at least kept me from despondency. Two or three of these I will now briefly mention.

"My own teacher is in many respects quite an interesting character.* He is a native of Shantung, a northern province, and of course speaks the Mandarin dialect. Part of his life has been spent at Peking in the service of the Russians there resident. 'He was 'born,' to use his own phraseology, 'a Romanist,' and has been carefully trained in Papal schools. He can sing, and talk bad Latin. His knowledge of the Scriptures is not inconsiderable, though mixed with many erroneous notions. In his feelings and tastes he sympathizes with foreigners. For some reason or other he became dissatisfied with the system in which he was educated, dismissed the idea of entering the priesthood for which he was destined, and came to Shanghai. There for the first time he heard the truth preached in its purity. His understanding responded to its claim; his heart also, it is to be hoped. About eight months ago he became my teacher. During all this time his mind has been brought into daily contact with the word of God. He has seen its

* Not the same spoken of in a former chapter.

authority appealed to as the basis of every belief and practice. The consequence is that his prejudices have gradually melted away. His errors have been corrected, and his mind enlightened.

"A few evenings since he told me of his own accord that he agreed with me on all subjects but two, the worship of the Virgin and Purgatory. About these he still felt some hesitation. I pointed to the Bible and asked him to produce its testimony in favor of these dogmas. He made no attempt to reply. I then set before him in a few words the common Protestant view, to the correctness of which he assented.

"For myself, as an individual, he professes the warmest attachment, and his mind is full of plans to promote my usefulness. One of these, which partakes largely of the nature of an 'air castle,' contemplates my removal to the vicinity of the imperial capital. According to his statements there would be a promising field of labor among multitudes of Romanists who are weary of the Papal yoke. More than once he has expressed a wish to be received to Christian fellowship, but I have as yet taken no step in that direction. There are still some inconsistencies in his views and conduct which excite suspicion of his sincerity. These may be due principally to the false notions imbibed in early youth. On the whole I cannot but hope that he will yet prove himself a decided Christian, and a valuable helper in diffusing the truth among his countrymen.

"A servant who has been with us about a year and a half, gives pleasing evidence of being affected by the truth. He appears to delight in all religious exercises, and gives the most fixed attention to the message of salvation. He often came to my room for instruction, and though naturally very ignorant and dull of apprehension, grew perceptibly in the knowledge of the gospel. The recovery of a son who was brought to the very gates of the grave, was made the means of deepening his interest in divine things. He still insists that the power and mercy of Jesus were directly displayed in the healing of the child. Two months since he requested baptism, but we felt constrained to defer the administration of that solemn rite till we have more decisive evidence of his conversion. At present he is with Mr. Burdon at Shanghai."

On the 29th of June, 1857, he again wrote:—*

"Since my last communication I have been permitted to prosecute my labors at Ping-Hoo without molestation from the authorities or the people. As eight or nine months have elapsed since we commenced our operations in that city, it might, perhaps, claim a place among the *stations* of the American Board. Just at present, however, nothing in China wears the aspect of certainty or permanence.

"Two individuals at Ping-Hoo, in addition to those mentioned in my last communication, have shown a decided interest in the truth. One of these was the father of the girl whose death I described three months ago. The story of the family is a sad one. Escaping from Nanking two years since, they were reduced to great straits. Want forced the parents to sell the younger of their two children, a girl eight or nine years of age. On the death of the older, their hearts doubly yearned after the little one from whom they had parted. The father being furnished with the necessary funds to redeem his child, (only eight dollars,) proceeded to Chang

* To the Mission House, from Shanghai.

Chow, where she was living. Weeks passed without tidings, and we began to be anxious. At last a letter and a bundle arrived, the former, in a strange hand, announcing his death, the latter containing his scanty wardrobe, with other articles of little value. He had been disappointed in his object, and had died, apparently as much from grief as from disease.

"I am not without hope that he was removed to a better world, where the wicked cease from troubling and the weary are at rest. For three months he resided in our house, hearing all our conversations with visitors, and regularly attending family worship. He acquired a fair knowledge of Bible truth, and professed his firm faith in Christ. Of his own accord he requested admission to the visible Church, and I intended to baptize him on his return. But God had otherwise planned. Perhaps we are too slow to recognize converts from among the people. I have taken measures to recover the child, and restore her to her widowed mother.

"The other case is that of a young man who was employed in a pawnbroker's establishment. He called upon us almost daily for months, and grew rapidly in his knowledge of the gospel, and apparent attachment to it. I hear that his employers have attempted to discourage his inclinations to the foreign doctrines. His conduct has furnished some pleasing evidence of his sincerity. At present he is on a visit to his native city, in a neighboring province. Before leaving he begged a number of Christian books for distribution among his heathen friends. If he returns, as he hopes to do after three months, with the same feelings and desires, I think he may be immediately baptized."

Near the last of October, Mr. Aitchison with a party of friends visited Ningpo, to attend the wedding of Mr. Burdon, and evidently enjoyed the trip very much. "A few days before the wedding," he says, in one of his familiar letters, "a party of us took a trip into the country to see some famous water-falls. We started at nine o'clock on Tuesday evening, and returned early Saturday morning. On Wednesday at daylight we found ourselves at the head of boat navigation. Taking chairs (the whole party except myself) we pursued our way among the most beautiful hill scenery to the place of our destination,

Tseen-chang-yon Waterfall, near Ningpo, China.

Five Years in China. P. 197.

called 'Snowy Valley,' where we arrived at two o'clock. After dinner we sallied forth for exploration, and came at once upon a cataract pouring over a perpendicular ledge of rock three hundred feet high. We crawled cautiously to the edge of the abyss, and with awe-stricken spirits gazed downwards. It was an hour of rich enjoyment; the sunlight just fading among the magnificent peaks that towered all around us, and the quiet brook gliding peacefully to the plunging point, held us enchained.

"The next morning four of us set out to visit the higher fall, (500 feet,) and were well repaid for our toil and drenching, for it was a rainy morning. Friday we returned by a nearer route to the foot of the mountain, where we embarked on bamboo rafts. Gliding pleasantly along at the foot of the hills, over the rocky bed of the stream, now deep, now shallow, beguiling the time by conversation and singing, we reached our boat at sunset, and started for Ningpo, where we landed early next morning.

"On such trips there are many little privations and hardships to which one must submit, but with good company they are delightful."

CHAPTER XIV.

Abandons Ping-Hoo—New Treaties—Death of his father-in-law, and of Mrs. Burdon.

AFTER all that had been accomplished, and all that had been hoped for, at Ping-Hoo, it was still found impracticable to retain the place, even as an out-station, because of the unsettled state of the country, and the loneliness of the situation. Having been compelled, as we have seen, to part with his tried friend and companion, Mr. Aitchison returned in the spring of 1858 to Shanghai, there to study and wait further developments of Providence, devoting himself in the mean time to such missionary service as the circumstances would permit. Having no chapel of his own, he held for a time a daily service in that which was under the care of Mr. Burdon, residing also in his family.

Although war had been raging all the time since he entered the country, yet now a new and more portentous cloud is rising. Misunderstandings with the French and English threaten a more serious outbreak than ever before. The rupture came, with increased disturbance and trouble. The whole country was excited, and further attempts to effect a settlement in the interior were necessarily held in abeyance. But busy as ever, Mr. Aitchison engaged in preaching as opportunity offered, making also brief excursions into the surrounding country, while the greater part of his time was spent in poring over that "infinite quantity," as he called it, the Chinese language and literature, intending thereby to lay up rich stores of knowledge for future use, when the right spot for him should be found.

"As a Chinese student," so wrote his friend Mr. Burdon, at a later day, "he was from the first enthusiastic, and his interest ended only with his life. His theory on this point was, that the first five years in China should be principally spent in study, with as much of actual missionary work as is consistent with that object; but that afterwards a missionary's time should be spent principally in preaching and diffusing the gospel among the people, with just as much of study as will be consistent with that. And he adopted this theory on the principle, that though death should be ever present to our minds, as possibly and even probably near, yet all our plans and works should generally be undertaken and carried out as though long years of usefulness were before us."

At length, in June, 1858, by the treaties of Tientsin, the country, so far as foreign war was concerned, was pacified; and, as all had anticipated, new facilities for the spread of the gospel were obtained. Indeed, beside giving access to no less than thirteen new ports for trade, the entire kingdom seemed to be at once opened to missionary labors; and as the wonderful intelligence was sent to England with all possible despatch, and thence flashed across the Atlantic by the submarine cable just laid, the two continents stood still for a moment and rejoiced together in the wonderful things God had thus wrought. Of this new state of things Mr. Aitchison speaks in the following language:—

"The treaties recently signed at Tientsin, between China on the one hand, and the four great powers of the West, England, France, Russia and the United States on the other, furnish matter for devout thankfulness to God. The prayers of some now bowing before the throne above, and of many still bearing the heat and burden of the day, are answered. A wide breach has been made in the wall of exclusiveness, which so long interposed a formidable barrier between the heralds of salvation and the perishing millions of this empire.

"We are not so sanguine as to suppose, that no obstacles lie in the path to the full attainment of the privileges above indicated. Imperial edicts cannot change the disposition of the masses, nor secure the integrity of officials. In planting the standard of the cross in regions hitherto unexplored, we must expect opposition and danger; must be prepared for exhibitions of contempt and hatred. Families, especially, will have to encounter rooted prejudice and aversion. But it is our deliberate opinion that the time for the occupation of the interior has now come, and that all difficulties will vanish before the power of faith and love.

"If, however, our right to enter in and take

possession of the *whole* land, in Christ's name, were allowed for the moment to be doubtful, there is still ground for an appeal to the churches to send us reinforcements, in this fact, that nine new ports, three on the coast, three on adjoining islands, and three on the great river Yang-tsz-kiang, are certainly opened to trade, and of course to the propagation of Christianity. One of these is in the extreme North, on the coast of Manchuria, with the climate of New England; another in the extreme South, on the Island of Hai-nan, with the climate of Cuba; and the rest are between these limits, presenting a variety of climate adapted to every sort of physical constitution, and a difference of population suited to every grade of mental culture."

Soon after the foregoing was written, Mr. Aitchison was again called to a double sorrow, the death of his venerated father-in-law, and of his new and valued friend, Mrs. Burdon, in whose house he had found a pleasant home. Of both these events he tenderly speaks as follows:—

[To L. R. A.]

"SHANGHAI, *Sept.* 1, 1858.

"MY DEAR L.:—Your letter, containing the sad intelligence of our beloved father's death, reached me day before yesterday. * * * His end, so free from pain and anxiety, befitted the calm and holy life he led, and singularly accorded with his often expressed views in regard to the most desirable mode of making the transition from earth to heaven.

"In contemplating all the circumstances of his departure we can hardly grieve. Why should we? Not surely for him who has reached that haven of rest toward which we are all steering, who has already vanquished the foes against which we are still struggling. Nature, I know, claims her right to weep. Let our tears, however, be mingled with thanksgiving for that grace which shone so conspicuous, even to the happy termination of that protracted pilgrimage. Let faith soar above the grave where the dust reposes, in the sure hope of a glorious resurrection, to that bright abode where the spirit already lives in the presence of God. What we misname death is in reality but the entrance into life, it is the portal of immortality.

'Is that a death-bed where the Christian lies?
Yes, but not his—'tis death itself that dies.'

* * * * * *

"And now, my dear L., I must tell you what a terrible blow has fallen on this house since I last wrote—Mrs. Burdon is *dead.* She passed away on the morning of August 16th, after (I may almost say) but a single day's illness. Her disease was a mild form of cholera. * * *

"She fell into a stupor about four hours before her death; but up to that time had continued in a calm and peaceful frame of mind, expressing the fullest confidence in the Redeemer, and the most perfect acquiescence in his will. Thus was the bridal succeeded by the burial in the short space of a few months. * * * *

"In Mrs. Burdon I have lost a most affectionate and gentle sister, and the Chinese a friend whose place will not soon be made good. But God has taken her; and he knows what was for her good, for ours, and for the good of this poor heathen people. In this, as in all other events, *his will be done.*"

CHAPTER XV.

Explorations North—Disturbed State of the Country—Again in Soo-Chow.

AMONG the excursions made by Mr. Aitchison after his return from Ping-Hoo, was one toward the north, with the design of reaching Tsi-nan, the capital of Shantung, a province whose population is 28,000,000. His faithful friend, Mr. Burdon, was his companion. "Our immediate object," says Mr. Aitchison, "is to explore the region for the benefit of missionary families who meditate a settlement in the interior, and to effect such a settlement for ourselves if we find it practicable. Two other brethren purpose to accompany us, at least a part of the way, Mr. John and Mr. Lee, both of the London Missionary Society." They started on the 5th of October, 1858, but found the country in so unsettled a condition that they were not able to proceed far. At every town they were carefully scrutinized by officials, and every manner of objection was made to their advancing, especially, as it was pretended, on account of their own safety. On the fourth day Mr. Aitchison wrote:—

"Putting together all that we have learned directly and indirectly, from the common people and from the officials, this much seems to be certain; that within a few days past the insurgents have shown great activity; have defeated the imperialists in one or more battles; are now besieging Lohoh, and threatening Yang-Chow; the communication between the north and south sides of the Great River is cut off, and local banditti are springing up in various directions. We have almost come to the conclusion that a further advance northward is for the present impracticable. To-morrow being the Sabbath, we shall remain quietly where we are. What will be our course on Monday remains to be seen. Meanwhile we commit ourselves, and our cause, to Him who worketh all things after the counsel of his own will. With God for our guide, we cannot go astray; with him for our protector, no evil can befal us."

On the sixth day, the city magistrate at Tan-

Yan, promised to send a man with them to see them safely to the bank of the Great River. The truth was, this individual was to be a spy upon their conduct; and thenceforth daily they encountered new difficulties, heard more and more of the unsettled state of things further north, were followed and closely watched by their spy-protector, visited in every place by the officials in great pomp, until on the seventh day they reached Chin-Kiang, an important walled city, upon the Yang-tsz-Kiang River, which after an obstinate resistance was captured by the British in 1842.

On reaching this city, they attempted at once to enter it, but were repulsed by the ever-present officials. After considerable perseverance, however, they obtained permission to enter in company with the officers themselves. "We at once jumped ashore," says Mr. Aitchison, "and were soon within the gates. Confusion and desolation reigned on every hand. Numbers of Manchoo soldiers were gathered in little knots in the neighborhood of the gate. They were well dressed and rather respectable in their appearance, each bearing a Manchoo character upon his outer garment, probably the same in signification as that which the Chinese carry, 'brave.'

"We passed down the main street some distance, turned to the right, then back till we reached the wall, along which we walked to the gate at which we had entered. A rather noisy crowd followed us all the way, notwithstanding occasional reprimands from our guides. The whole place seemed to be in ruins. The few houses left standing were for the most part unoccupied. The shops open were principally those which dealt in provisions. Workmen were busy strengthening the defenses on the wall. Everything indicated that an attack was expected. On approaching the gate on our return, a short, ill-natured looking personage stepped from an office and whispered to our attendants, 'They must set sail at once.' This seemed only the expression of a general feeling on our part. Most of those around us appeared like villains ready for any desperate deed. With many thanks to our Mandarin friends, who had treated us with such real kindness, we stepped into our boat, and in a very short time were hastening away.

"It is pleasant to reflect that we have taken a

stroll in the city whose name has, for the last six years, resounded through the whole civilized world, and which I believe is destined to be the scene of yet other conflicts in the not remote future. A glance at its position shows that it is indeed the key of China, commanding so effectually both the Yang-tsz-Kiang, and the Grand Canal. Here the English forces met with a courageous and determined resistance in the last war, and here the same enemies may again try their strength."

They visited Kyin-Tan, Lih-Yang, Woosih, and Soo-Chow, and, after an absence of twenty days, returned safely to Shanghai. Of Lih-Yang Mr. Aitchison wrote:—"The dialect seems to be quite unlike the Shanghai on the one hand, and the Mandarin on the other. Probably we were the first foreigners that ever entered this city in European costume." At Woosih he said, "There has been much deliberation respecting our future course. My own way seems at present completely hedged up. Another attempt to reach the north by Chin-Kiang seems impracticable, and the outside passage, in a Chinese junk, against the monsoon, is no more feasible. Per-

18 *

haps I can do nothing better than to aid in preparing the way for the occupation of some of these cities of this neighborhood."

At Soo-Chow he wrote:—"The people did not seem surprised at our presence. A few individuals, chiefly of tender years, followed us about from street to street. We were everywhere hailed with the opprobrious appellation, 'Pah-que-tsz,' (foreign devils.) It is plain, however, that China is fast opening. It was in this very city, that on my first trip, four years ago, I was kept a prisoner one day, and then sent back to Shanghai under an escort. Then it was not considered safe to enter it except in disguise. Now we go in freely, and no one offers to hinder or molest us. Let us hope the day is near when missionary families will occupy this important position, and churches of Christ will flourish among its godless and pleasure-loving population."

A month later he was again in that great and interesting city, and wrote as follows:—

"My little boat has been successively anchored at each of the six gates, and I have daily traversed the crowded thoroughfares, in every direction, without let or hindrance. My brief experience proves that a great change has been effected in the native policy within the last few years. Only a little more than twelve months ago foreigners were turned back from these gates, and a degree of hostility was exhibited by the people, which is rare in this part of China. My message has been listened to with great apparent interest by the various audiences which have been addressed.

"But oh! how powerless I feel myself to be in the midst of such a multitude! Only think of some poor stranger anchored at the foot of Wall Street, in New York, speaking the English language but imperfectly, and yet designing to introduce a new religion among its busy population. Such in a human point of view is the undertaking in which I am at present embarked. Surely I have infinite reason to commit my cause to God, and depend upon him alone. With him is the residue of the Spirit, and that Divine Agent can subdue the proud heart even of a Chinaman.

"As yet my labors are confined to the simple proclamation of the gospel. Taking my stand in any convenient place, either by the way-side or the steps of some temple, I do not need to wait long for an audience. People flock in from every direction anxious to see the barbarian. Beginning with a few simple inquiries by way of conciliation, I gradually turn the conversation to religion, and then deliver a formal address, occasionally, however, putting a question, by way of testing their knowledge, and keeping alive their interest. It is a very encouraging fact that almost every such assemblage of hearers has a few who give the strictest attention to all that is said. Priests from neighboring temples are often among the hearers.

"Mr. Blodget has been with me to-day; we have had a delightful day preaching together, each of us having addressed a congregation at least six times.

"My immediate object here is to open the way for the permanent residence of some missionary families. To this end I go into the city daily that the people may become accustomed to the sight of foreigners. Of course I get abundantly hooted at by fellows of the baser sort, but this does me no harm. I am according to their language sometimes a 'foreign devil,' sometimes a 'white devil,' sometimes a 'black devil,' and sometimes simply 'devil.' Perhaps you would like to know how I rebuke such persons. Generally I do not notice it, especially if it come from the lower class of the people. If those who appear respectable use the epithet maliciously, occasionally I rebuke them sharply, telling them that they have no manners, which often brings the blush to their faces. At other times I tell them that Confucius, their great sage, said, 'All men are brothers;' now if you and I are brothers, and I am really a devil, what then are *you?* This often turns the laugh upon them, and makes them slip away out of sight."

A CHINESE IDOL RECEIVING WORSHIP.

CHAPTER XVI.

Bright Prospects—Suddenly clouded—Death of Mr. Macy—Again Bewildered.

THE year 1859 opened with bright prospects to the missionaries in China. Nothing was indeed directly said in the new treaties about the residence of missionaries in the interior towns and cities, but it was fully believed that what the Government would not in *words* permit, they would not in *fact* prevent. It was therefore felt that an entirely new era was about to dawn on China, and all looked anxiously forward to see how they should enter upon it. Each mission began to look to its resources, and to calculate on its share of labors and results in the new field.

None was in a better position to take advantage of this new state of things than that of the American Board. Two of its missionaries were indeed needed in Shanghai, one engaged in the translation of the Scriptures, and one in direct labors among the people; but beside these there were two others, whose presence in that city did not seem necessary, and who had special reasons for seeking other fields. Both were in the prime of life and in the strength of their manhood; both single, and ready, therefore, the better to face many of the inconveniences, difficulties, and dangers of a new enterprise. Both indeed had been for some time preparing to plant the gospel in some city north of the Yang-tsz-Kiang, and in that direction their thoughts were now turned.

These men were Mr. Aitchison and the Rev. William Allen Macy. The latter had previously been connected with the mission at Ningpo, but had joined that at Shanghai, because of the disturbed condition of things at the former port, rendering missionary labor more difficult and less promising than could be desired. These men were not strangers; they had long known each other, and were well fitted by common loveliness of character, by ripe scholarship, both in the European and the Chinese sense of the term; by devoted attachment to the missionary work, to be true yoke-fellows, and eminently qualified to be the pioneers of Protestant missions in regions where Christ had not been named.

And now also the ardent desire which Mr. Aitchison had so long cherished that he might effect a permanent residence somewhere in the interior, might find indeed a more promising field of labor than any he had yet seen, seemed about to be realized. He had, in fact, turned his longing eyes to the grand capital itself, hoping that he might some day get within its sacred walls, and even there "where Satan's seat is," have the unspeakable honor and privilege of planting the standard of the cross. Or, if he could not reach the capital, he had thought that Tung-Chow, a large city only twelve miles from Peking, might be his residence. For this purpose he had studied the Mandarin dialect, and held himself in readiness. "Speak, Lord, for thy servant heareth"—this was his waiting attitude, as it is always the glory of the creature.

So he and Mr. Macy were planning all the earlier part of the year, and fully expected to be able to start on their new and interesting expedition by the middle or end of April. But the Master had other plans for his servants; and never was the motto, "Man proposes; God disposes," more strikingly exemplified. Before the April showers began to fall, Mr. Macy was prostrated by sudden sickness, which proved to be confluent small-pox in its worst form. For eleven days Mr. Aitchison watched most tenderly over the sick, did all in his power to minister to his comfort, bathing his eyes and face during the violence of the disease, reading to him, and praying with him; and when death had done its work, with Mr. Blodget, he prepared the poor mortal remains for the tomb.

To Mr. Aitchison this new dispensation of Providence seemed dark indeed. He knew not what it meant, or which way to turn. Writing to his beloved friend Mr. Burdon he says:—

"Thus, once more my cherished hopes are dashed, and my favorite plans frustrated. I trust, however, I am able to look up, and say to God, in this dispensation, as in all others, 'Not my will, but thine be done.' If years of labor are still allotted me, as on the whole I anticipate, I know not at present what course to steer. My aspirations are still interiorwards, either in the direction of the north or west. Should some happy turn of Providence make your path and mine coincident, I should esteem myself highly favored. Doubtless the Lord will order our steps aright, if we sincerely look to him for guidance."

In the same letter he reviews his past connection with China, and dedicates himself anew to his Master. "This is the anniversary of my sailing from America. Five years ago, just at this hour of noon, the good ship Candace cast loose from the wharf, and turned her prow toward the far east.

"Truly goodness and mercy have followed me during all this time. How much occasion I have for gratitude and praise! And yet how little have I accomplished in the cause of my Lord and Master! It is high time to gird on my armor anew; it is high time to enter in earnest upon the conflict with the powers of darkness, both in me and around me. Do, my dear brother, lend me the aid of your prayers."

Attending upon a friend in that fearful disease as Mr. Aitchison did, was not, of course, without serious exposure of his own life; but God was merciful, and he was spared. And yet, breathing, for eleven successive nights and parts of days, the pestilential air of such a sick room, together with the fatigue of protracted watching, had sensibly affected his health.

THE CHINESE SEDAN CHAIR.

CHAPTER XVII.

Still Planning—Joins the Embassy to Peking—Repulse at the Peiho—Negotiations and Hopes.

STILL hoping that some kind providence would prepare the way for his access to some one of the Northern provinces, or to the capital itself, early in June Mr. Aitchison most unexpectedly received an invitation to join, as one of its interpreters, the American Embassy, then about to proceed to Peking. This seemed to be the very thing for which, in substance, he had been so long waiting and praying. It would at least give him an opportunity to explore the country; and if he found it possible to remain in the Capital, and be the first to live and labor as a true missionary of the cross, in that great centre of the most populous kingdom of the globe, he would consider himself the most favored and most happy man on earth.

With some hope at least of this sort, and feeling also that the trip might be beneficial to his health, he readily accepted the invitation tendered him, and, singularly enough, parted from his dear friends in Shanghai as though he did not expect to meet them again this side of the throne of God. The Embassy, consisting of his excellency, Mr. Ward, Minister Plenipotentiary from this country, with his suite, embarked on the 16th of June, in the U. S. frigate Powhatan, attended by a smaller steamer, the Taiwan, and was five days sailing up the coast. In that brief period Mr. Aitchison had manifestly improved in health and spirits. But on reaching the mouth of the Peiho, the expedition was brought to a sudden and unexpected stand by the unlooked for defeat of the French and English, by the Chinese, of which Mr. Aitchison, not without some personal danger, was a spectator.

For several days after this disastrous repulse all was confusion and disappointment. The English were trying to get away their disabled gunboats, whilst the Chinese kept up a steady fire from their forts, and poor, weary, worn stragglers were coming in. We give some of Mr. Aitchison's reflections, the first written at the close of the Sabbath succeeding the repulse.

"Such have been the scenes of this holy day. Never did I spend one like it, and it is my earnest prayer that I may never spend another in similar circumstances. War never appeared to me so horrible as it does now. Oh, when will the Prince of Peace extend his peaceful sway over the earth, and the nations learn war no more!"

After giving a more minute account of the "immediate *occasion* of this tremendous conflict," Mr. Aitchison says: "Its effects, for some time to come, will be exceedingly prejudicial to the interests of foreigners, but doubtless the final result will be for good. The day of retribution will surely come, and when it does the English will not be satisfied with the privileges guaranteed by the now annulled treaty, but they will demand far more. Of course we have given up all hope of reaching Peking this year. What the course of events will be it is impossible to determine.

"I tremble for the infant missions, already established under favorable circumstances at Hang-Chow and elsewhere. Probably the tidings of yesterday's defeat will lead to their temporary abandonment. Thus ends the treaty of Tientsin, which thrilled the Christian world with joy and hope. All our fondest anticipations are disappointed. The gloom which was just beginning to disperse from this land has settled down with increasing density, and all the bright future is clouded. It is a comfort to know that God reigns. His time will come sooner or later, and then, without doubt, there will be a glorious display of infinite grace."

The following incident will be noticed with interest.

"June 28. Another bright and beautiful day. Had a long conversation with a young Jew, who is serving on board as a common sailor. I had heard of him through Mr. Wood, the chaplain. He can speak several modern languages, and appears to have a fair English education. He was born in Bavaria, but has resided for many years in the United States. Losses in business drove him to sea. He told me that the other sailors were always ridiculing his efforts to improve his mind; and therefore he was compelled to write and read late in the evening, when his messmates had retired. Because of this bantering he had destroyed two volumes of a journal which he had been keeping. 'Now,' said he, 'I write in Chaldean, and that is a language which they cannot understand.'

"Gradually I drew him into a conversation upon Christianity, and he spoke candidly about his Jewish faith. He professes to have examined the claims of Jesus to be the Messiah, and yet remains unconvinced. I tried to set before him some of the evidences of Jesus' Messiahship, and he listened with great apparent interest. I hope to have other opportunities for conversation with him before leaving the ship."

The journal of "June 30th," mentions some interesting incidents:—"Within the last three days several bodies of foreigners have floated by. Poor fellows! who knows what mother or sister or wife may suffer when the sad tidings of last Saturday's defeat reach England's happy homes! Many hearts will bleed, and ask, why all this bloodshed.

"One thing worth mentioning is the lowness of the barometer at this anchorage. Although the weather has been fine, the mercury seldom rises above 29° 60′. Once or twice it sank so low that a storm was anticipated, but rose again without any wind. Frequent gusts of wind, some of them amounting to a squall, sweep over our anchorage, lashing the sea into a sudden fury, and then abruptly ceasing.

"Our chief annoyance is the flies. The cabin is full of them. They crawl into one's ears and eyes and mouth and nostrils. At meals they take their full share of everything on the table. They wake us at daylight every morning, and then keep us awake as effectually as any alarm clock. Huc speaks of sparrows as the cosmopolites of the feathered tribes. The flies seem to be the cosmopolites of the insect creation.

"July 5. Just at dusk a note was put into my hands by an orderly. Its contents gave me more pure pleasure than I can express. The young Jew mentioned June 28th is the writer. A few extracts will exhibit his spiritual state. 'Since those perfect, true words which you had the kindness to communicate to me my whole system has undergone an entire change. Although born, raised and educated in the religion of my forefathers, and always firmly believing in the precepts which their experience has shown me, I begin now, and only since my conversation with you, to believe that there is still something missing to fill that cup of blessedness in the human soul, which only pure and true religion can bestow. Certainly, sir, I do not mean to bring into consideration any worldly enjoyments whatsoever, for my firm belief is that not a small portion of heavenly peace is wanted for the performance of a peaceable pilgrimage through this vale of tears. Encouraged by your good advice, I found that the wants of a peaceable existence for me have been the faith and true belief in the true religion.

"'I therefore declare to you hereby openly, with my own free will and accord, that the heavenly arrow aimed by you at my spiritual eye, has come home to its place of destination, and that the veil of doubts which overhangs my mind has totally vanished, and I perceive nothing but a true shining light in the word of the Saviour of mankind.'

"I do not feel prepared to pass my opinion upon this letter or its author at present. I will have further conversation with the young man before I give him my full confidence.

"July 6th. This evening had a long and interesting conversation with the young Jew mentioned yesterday. So far as I can judge, he is sincere in his professions of faith in Jesus, as the Messiah, the Son of God. Of course his views of many subjects are vague and ill-defined. He is reading the New Testament, and is rejoiced to find how exactly Christ answers to the predictions of the Old. I exhorted him to pray much for spiritual enlightenment, and he promised to do so."

CHAPTER XVIII.

Conference with the Governor—Arrangements Completed—Journey to the Capital.

SEVERAL days were now spent in getting the royal permission from Peking for the contemplated visit of the Embassy, and in making the preliminary arrangements. In one of the interviews on shore, where these matters were discussed, there was present a young Chinese, who sat near the chief speaker, but took no part in the deliberations. He had been educated in the Episcopal Mission at Shanghai, had been to England and America, and of course could understand and speak the languages of the barbarians. The year before he had gone up there with Mr. Wade, but left him at Tientsin to enter the service of his country. Three days later the young man came out and visited the Americans. Of this interview Mr. Aitchison writes,—"Once on shipboard he threw off much of his former reserve,

A friendly party in China.

Five Years in China. P. 228.

and I had a long and interesting conversation with him in English. He talks the language of Canaan, and I cannot but hope that a spark of grace has been kindled in his heart. In his present situation he is compelled to be very cautious. The least imprudence might cost him his head. He hopes to accomplish much in bringing his countrymen to adopt both the civilization and the religion of Western nations.

"In speaking of the Trinity, a subject which came up while noticing the difference between the Roman and the Greek churches, he employed the following illustration. The Son is like the *flame* which you *see*, the Father is like the *substance* from which the flame *proceeds*, the Spirit is like the *heat* which you *feel* but cannot see. Though this language fails to express the real distinction in the persons of the Godhead, it is still rather remarkable as coming from a Chinese in such circumstances. For a year he has had no intercourse with any foreigner, nor does he dare to keep by him any book produced in the West. With ill-suppressed anxiety he proposed the inquiry, 'On what conditions will the English be likely to make peace with us under existing cir-

20

cumstances?' Mr. Martin expressed my own opinion in replying, 'Only by removing the barriers at the mouth of the Pei-ho and permitting at least two gun-boats to proceed, with their minister, to Tientsin.' A letter of introduction from Mr. Syle of Shanghai, which one of the officers presented to him, he did not dare to keep, but requested me to carry it back to its author, and beg him to preserve it till under other circumstances he could safely receive it.

"July 17. Sabbath. To-day, instead of the sermon at the time of the service, we had a missionary meeting, Dr. Williams, Mr. Martin, and myself being the speakers. I commenced with a statement of the moral and religious condition of China without the gospel; Mr. Martin followed with some facts illustrating the success of missionary labors even in this empire; and Dr. Williams closed by contrasting the present aspect of the work with what it was when he arrived here twenty-six years ago. The chaplain expressed his satisfaction with the meeting, and it is to be hoped that many will remember what was said, and profit thereby.

"July 18. This evening had another interesting

conversation with the young Jew. He tells me there are one or two of his shipmates who are more or less interested in the subject of religion. It would be worth while to have undertaken the present journey, if even one immortal soul should thereby receive serious impressions which should result in conversion."

At last the arrangements for the embassy were completed. Twenty-five chariots were provided for the land journey, five of which were to be of a superior kind, for Mr. Ward, the Commodore, and other chief members of the expedition. On reaching the river, a distance of forty miles, a sufficient number of boats were to be in readiness, three of which were to be larger than the rest. Two officers were appointed to conduct the Embassy to the capital. On the morning of the 20th of July they started, the company consisting of twenty foreigners, three Chinese scribes, and seven Chinese servants.

"Once out of the village," says Mr. Aitchison, "we entered a country perfectly flat and barren. As far as the eye could see, there was nothing to break the monotony except the grave-mounds. For several miles there was visible hardly a blade of grass. Here we met a party of cavalry galloping in the direction of Pehtang. They eyed us curiously as they passed. Each warrior seemed to form a component part of the animal he rode. Across his back was slung a match-lock, and at the saddle-bow his knapsack. Some carried bow and arrows, others pistols, and still others swords. The next few miles presented a more agreeable appearance, being covered with green grass and weeds, but there were no signs of cultivation. On we rode over this dreary waste, sometimes sinking a foot deep in the sticky mud.

"Each chariot was drawn by two stout mules in the manner we call *tandem*, except that the forward mule keeps a little to the right of the hind one, and the traces are attached to the wagon just in front of the axle-tree. The driver sits in the front of the carriage, with his feet dangling down almost to the ground. He is busily occupied almost the whole time either in beating his team or shouting at them. In his right hand he flourishes a whip with a handle at least five feet long, and a lash to correspond.

"Our caravan presented quite a picturesque appearance as it wound over the grassy plain.

Scattered here and there among the chariots were Chinese officers on horse-back, who galloped back and forth as occasion required, their red hair plumes floating away behind the conical caps which the rites compel them to wear. About noon we arrived at a village called Kiunliang-choong, where by previous arrangement we were to eat our noon-day meal. Numbers of officers small and great welcomed us, and in a very short time we were busily employed in disposing of a most sumptuous dinner. There was no end to meats, vegetables, and fruits.

"I am happy to say that before night closed in, a great transformation had taken place in the feelings and opinions of many of our party. Hitherto they have regarded the Chinese with the utmost aversion, believing them guilty of every vice, and destitute of every virtue. This single day's experience has convinced them of their mistake. They are ready to confess that the Chinese have many qualities which render them worthy of respect and affection. The kindness we have received certainly could not well be surpassed. All the arrangements proved their desire to gratify our tastes in every particular. Inscriptions were pasted over the doors and on the walls which indicate the sentiments entertained toward us. Among these, many of which are difficult of translation, were the following:—

"In large characters opposite the principal entrance were the words, 'Great Joy!' On a door, 'Receive all Heavenly Happiness!' On the sides of the door were two sentences, the literal translation of which was, 'Felicitous Sun, auspicious clouds,' and 'Harmonious breezes, sweet rains.' Over another door was written, 'Happiness comes from heaven!' On the opposite side of another, 'Imagination, like a great dragon, soars a hundred feet,' and 'Literature, like a good horse, is vigorous a thousand autumns.' Another pair of sentences, perfectly Chinese, was, 'The virtue of sages is like sweet wine; Heaven's grace enriches;' and, 'The words of a king are like silken sounds; the kingdom's favors are many!'

"We spent the entire afternoon in conversing with our escort, and strolling about in the immediate neighborhood. The whole hamlet had the appearance of a fair. Carts were standing in every direction, the mules feeding close by. Numbers of soldiers were guarding the baggage, and were anxious to guard us in all our rambles. At last, to our extreme relief, evening came, and our official and officious friends left us to ourselves. We made up our beds in the various apartments that had been assigned to us, and at an early hour retired. Mr. Wood and myself had poor accommodations, but we got some doors for bedsteads and slept tolerably well.

"July 21. At daylight we were stirring, and by six o'clock on our road to Peitsang, or, 'Northern Granary,' where we take boats for Tung-Chow, which is distant from Peking only twelve miles. In the course of the morning we passed a number of small villages, the houses being universally built of mud, but so skillfully put together that many of them were very neat in appearance. At half past nine we reached a village called Si-ti-teu, where another sumptuous entertainment, and a number of officers, awaited our arrival. After resting here for nearly two hours, we again set forth, and about the middle of the afternoon arrived at the 'Northern Granary,' where a number of yellow flags directed us to the spot where we embark in the boats.

"This day's travel has been very trying to

many of our party. Certainly none of us ever received a jolting to compare with that which fell to our lot during these last few hours. The road is in a most terrible condition, in many places flooded with water to the depth of a foot. The face of the country closely resembles that of the prairie-land of the far west, except that the grass is shorter, and there are no flowers. The poor mules had a hard time of it. Once mine lay down flat in the midst of the mud and water, completely exhausted, and frequently he seemed just on the point of falling. We passed a few small hamlets which generally bear the name of the principal family residing there. The poor people lined the road to gaze upon us as we passed. They are not very prepossessing at first sight, but I presume would improve upon acquaintance. Assuredly I have seen nothing during these two days to lead to the desire of spending my life here, rather than at the south. Well may the poor wretches whose lives are passed on the plains speak of Soochow, and Hang-Chow as Paradise, and yet the climate is delightful; the atmosphere is clear and bracing, and the people seem contented with their apparently hard lot.

"During these two days we have traveled about one hundred and sixty *li*, or fifty miles. We now learn for the first time that this place is above Tientsin about ten miles. It seems plain that great pains have been taken to prevent us from visiting that city. The reason is easy to conjecture. Probably the Chinese are unwilling to allow any foreigners to inspect the military defences of the place. Doubtless their renowned warrior, Sung-ko-lin-sin, has been spending his energies principally in fortifying that neighborhood.

"The transference of ourselves and our luggage from the chariots to the boats was the cause of as much hubbub and annoyance as our start from the northern entrance. All felt rather disappointed at the first sight of the boats destined to be our abode for the next few days. There are only five in all, three large ones and two small, none of them very respectable in external appearance or internal arrangements.

"July 22. At daylight the gongs sounded the signal for departure, and in an instant all was noise and apparent confusion on every boat of our little fleet. Sleep was an impossibility, and therefore most of us rose to enjoy the scene. It was not long before we were fairly under way, the boats following each other in lines on both sides of the stream. The boats of our escort are far more numerous, but smaller than our own. Each is drawn by a number of men who march on the bank. At the mast-head of that occupied by his excellency, floats the beautiful silk flag belonging to the legation. In the afternoon the yellow flag of the Imperial Government was also hoisted to the same height, and they flaunted together in the breeze till night-fall.

"The river is about seventy-five yards wide. It is now quite full, with a very strong current, the water being thick with mud. The banks are low, and the adjacent country under good cultivation. No hills or undulations are visible. Among the chief productions I noticed millet, small rice, (also a species of millet,) hemp, maize, sweet potatoes, and almost every variety of ordinary garden vegetables. We passed many villages, and one large town called Yang-tsun. The houses, with a very few exceptions, are built of mud. In numerous places the banks were lined with eager multitudes, gazing with bursting sockets upon the strangers. There was, however, no noise or confusion among them. The dress of but few individuals indicated scholarship or wealth, but most seemed well fed and cheerful. At Yang-tsun preparations had been made for an interchange of visits between our minister and his escort, but the crowd was so great that the ceremony was dispensed with, and we proceeded after a halt of less than five minutes.

"Shortly after rising we had a visit in our boat from Li-Lan-Ye, the third officer of our escort. He is an easy, jolly, good-natured fellow, not overburdened with knowledge, either of foreign countries or his own. He drank a cup of coffee and smoked a cigar with great apparent gusto. Like most of our visitors he especially admired the opera-glasses, and never tired of looking through them. At breakfast we found ourselves minus all the articles considered indispensable to that meal, but we at last managed to get a little rice, a few eggs and a cup of coffee. I then jumped ashore for a walk, and as was anticipated, a couple of petty officers soon joined me. Remonstrance was in vain. They had received orders from the 'great man' to escort and protect me from the stupid people, and they must obey. I, however, continued and enjoyed my walk, without the least annoyance from the people. A garden laid out quite in foreign style particularly attracted my attention. Water was conveyed to it from the river by means of a sort of windlass. I saw on the bank a sign board which, in addition to the common assurance of entertainment for man and beast, informed the public that the keeper of the establishment was of the Western Mohammedan faith.

"It pleases me exceedingly to watch the changes taking place in the feelings and opinions of some of my traveling companions. Most of them are delighted beyond measure with every thing they see. Japan begins to fade in their vision.

"Once or twice to-day we passed places where evidently preparations had been made to barricade the river in case the English should make an attempt on the capital. Immense logs were laid in order on the banks, and according to the information of the boatmen, such was the use for which they were designed.

"A striking thing in the landscape was the

number of mules, horses, donkeys, and cows. They are grazing about in every direction. On the roads, which are slightly elevated above the general level, horsemen and carts are constantly passing, sometimes singly, and sometimes in small caravans.

"July 23. Nothing new in the scenery has presented itself except a range of blue mountains in the distance. I have been unable to ascertain either their name or their position. Some persous tell me they are beyond the Great Wall, but that can hardly be possible. By compass they lie to the north-east of us. We cannot but wish that our road lay along their base. The landscape adjoining the river is indeed interesting, but monotonous.

"July 24. Sunday. This day has had but little of a Sabbath aspect. The countrymen work equally hard on the banks, the crowd assemble to gaze, and the coolies make the same noise as on ordinary days. Oh, when will a New England or Scottish Sabbath dawn on this vast empire? The work is one of the greatest magnitude. Truly nothing but Omnipotence can accomplish it.

"Though slowly approaching the capital, the

country does not improve in any respect; the banks are low, the villages are few, and the people as poor as in the neighborhood of Tientsin. Indeed nothing indicates our proximity to one of the chief cities of the world, unless it be the number of grain-bearing junks which we pass every few hours. These go in fleets, one of which, I learned, had been about *four* months on the road from Ho-nan.

"July 25. Yesterday and to-day we have been favored with showers of rain which have contributed to keep the atmosphere at a delightful temperature. The scenery on the banks offers nothing worthy of special remark. The same blue hills lie in the distance, changing their direction to every point of the compass, as we follow the windings of the river.

"Frequently the stream almost doubles back upon itself, so that the first boat sees the last one on its bow.

"July 26. Early in the morning, and two or three times during the day, we passed barriers consisting of several rows of piles driven into the river from bank to bank, only leaving a narrow passage for junks. Some of our boatmen affirm that the object of these is to defend the Imperial grain vessels from the ice in winter, others to prevent the approach of an enemy, (*i. e.* the English) toward the capital. The land adjacent to the river has not risen perceptibly during these two days, though it seems better wooded than before. We have passed many fleets of Imperial junks laden with grain, principally rice, wheat, and beans. These have come from the central provinces, and have been three or four months on their way. Each fleet consists of about twenty vessels, and is guarded by a petty officer with a few soldiers.

"We have been much interested in seeing our boat-trackers devour the humble meals which are furnished them. I have seen no meat on their table. They seem to eat only ground millet made into a sort of porridge or cake, and a little vegetable as an accompaniment. We ourselves have had this millet porridge served up to us for breakfast, and we all pronounced it little inferior to that made from maize.

"To our great satisfaction the Tung-Chow pagoda became visible about the middle of the afternoon, this being about the fifth day from Pehtsang. It was not, however, until after dark that we reached the jetty prepared for a landing-place. Our boats were all anchored side by side, though the operation was accompanied with a great uproar. Bronchitis seems to be a rare disease among Chinese boatmen, especially here at the North. The evening has been spent in making preparations for our land journey of twelve miles, and all of us are anticipating with lively interest the event of to-morrow."

CHAPTER XIX.

In the Capital—Virtual Prisoners—Speculations—A few Keepsakes.

"July 27. PEKING! Here we are, at last, in the capital of the largest empire of the earth. We entered the gate at precisely two o'clock, and arrived at the house prepared for our residence at a quarter before three.

"We left the boats near the eastern gate of Toong-chow at seven o'clock after a hasty but excellent breakfast. Our chariots with single mules were arranged on the bank in the order of precedence. The very sight of these vehicles caused the bones of the stoutest among us to ache. However as there was no other resource, we were soon jogging along the stone road which conducts the traveler through Toong-chow to Peking. We entered the east, and soon emerged from the west gate of this inferior department. I was struck with the badness of the road, the fineness of the shops, and the frequency of the taverns.

Multitudes lined the road as our cavalcade moved onwards. Once fairly in the city, I leaped from my cart, and advanced on foot. The people made no noise or disturbance. Few followed me even for a short distance, but all gazed with open eyes and mouth.

"Having passed out of the west gate we found ourselves upon a broad causeway, elevated two or three feet above the surrounding country, paved with stones, most of which were about four feet long, two and a half wide, and one foot thick. These were broken in many places, and worn away in others, so that the carriages seemed ready to overturn or break in pieces at every foot of their progress. Within a very few minutes most of the embassy had vacated their close carts, and were either pedestrianizing or jogging along on little donkeys hired from men who chanced to be proceeding in the same direction, and thus we advanced almost to the suburbs of the great city.

"The surrounding country offered a very pleasing prospect, being diversified not indeed with hill and valley, but with clumps of trees, fields of millet, ornamental pavilions, honorary gateways, sepulchres, hamlets, and all the other accompaniments of an ordinary Chinese landscape. On the road itself there was much to interest us. We either met or overtook multitudes going to, or coming from the capital. There were lines of camels carrying either coal or grain, ugly from the want of hair, the breadth of their feet, and their awkward manner of carrying their heads and necks. There were wheelbarrows laden with bags of refuse from the hemp plant, after the oil has been pressed from its beans, some drawn by donkeys and some pushed by men; there were donkeys, and mules and horses, with their variously dressed riders, passing at every rate of speed to and fro. There too were our escort, mounted on fine animals, the tails of biped and quadruped alike floating in the gentle breeze.

"From the neighboring hamlets, multitudes flocked to see the passing show, among them not a few damsels, whose large feet betrayed their Tartar origin. The day has been intensely hot, though clouds favored us with their leaden screens. Now and then we halted under a wayside tree, and drank the pure cool water freshly drawn from a neighboring well or spring. For half an hour we all halted for tea and refreshments at an old Monastery, called Monastery of the Compassionate Clouds. The priests received us cordially and entertained us hospitably, setting before us tea, watermelons, and Indian corn boiled in the ear. From this point many of our party proceeded on horse-back, or mule-back, or donkey-back, to the next halting-place, about three miles from the city gate, where our cavalcade was to form in regular order for entering the city.

"During the last stage of our journey we were the center of attraction to tens of thousands of gaping spectators. The avenue by which we approached the gate is certainly in many respects worthy of its place. At least a hundred feet wide, it is lined with magnificent shops, with here and there an honorary portal interspersed. One of these portals was of immense proportions, and elaborately carved and decorated. But the city gate itself, and the stupendous tower or bastion-like structure which surmounts it, quite surpassed my expectations. The adjoining wall too is very imposing in its height and apparent solidity. The space between the first and second entrance of the gate is quite spacious, and is perfectly com manded by the towers over both. The whole is built of large blue-colored bricks.

"There was a delay of a few minutes just before we passed through the second entrance. My heart beat quick at the very possibility of being stopped just as the dream of years was on the point of realization. But no! after a few horsemen had hurried past, and the policemen had flourished their whips *around* the shoulders of the eager and too forward spectators, the cavalcade was again in motion, and we passed amid a rush of exciting thoughts into the *real, genuine* PEKING.

"One of the first objects that attracted my attention was a Russian seated on his horse in the thickest of the crowd. Though dressed in European costume, his presence seemed to excite no surprise. Perhaps our cavalcade divided the attention which otherwise might have been paid to him. After a ride of a little more than a mile in the city, we reached our present abode. Our quarters are capacious and airy, but not very well furnished. The apartments are all on the ground floor. The principal court-yard is shaded with matting laid upon a framework erected over it. This shades the area below, and contributes greatly to our comfort.

"Until night closed in, all of us were busily occupied in attending to the luggage, and arranging our apartments. Mr. Martin and myself have secured a quiet, retired room quite removed from the noise and bustle of the 'dusty world,' and here we hope to spend many a pleasant hour of our sojourn in the capital. Quite a sense of relief stole over us as soon as our premises were fairly vacated by the score of officials who had been surrounding us from the hour we set out this morning. We had our usual season of social prayer before retiring to rest, and I trust felt emotions of true gratitude on reviewing the way by which God has led us since leaving Shanghai.

"July 28. The officers of every grade have left us to ourselves during the entire day. Not one of them has been near us. There have been various opinions expressed on their motives in this line of conduct. The explanation that most accords with my own opinion and feeling is, that our friends with true delicacy wish to give us a fair opportunity to rest and recruit ourselves after the fatigues of our recent journey. Some think that they are puzzled to know how to treat us, and are taking time for thought and deliberation. I can easily believe that our recent escort and our Shanghai friends, Kwei-liang and Hwa-sha-na, who arrived three days ago, have been taking counsel together both respecting the past, present and future. We are all curious to know the line of policy which is to be pursued. I trust it will be a liberal and not a restrictive one. After coming so far, it would be a pity to return without seeing some of the wonders which such a city must present to the eye of a stranger from the west.

"Chinese servants abound in all parts of our premises. They are respectful and tolerably efficient. It is to be hoped the result will prove them to be honest. Mr. Martin and myself have two set apart for our special accommodation. They sit outside of our door by day and sleep there by night. Anything we want done, they are prompt to attend to it. Others are stationed in each court-yard ready for any summons.

"Everything we desire in the way of provisions is promptly furnished on our requisition. Each evening a list of articles is to be handed to the purveyor-general, and the next morning they will be forthcoming. Two things which are luxuries in China can be obtained here in abundance, viz: ice and milk. The latter article is in extensive use among the Tartars.

"This day has been very sultry, although the thermometer has only risen to 85°. Most of the gentlemen have been making every effort to keep cool, but without much success. On examining the position of our quarters, I find that they are situated in the north-east corner of the inner city, in a lane called 'Old Prince Hall;' or No. 13. This edifice formerly belonged to an imperial subject, but was afterwards confiscated to the government.

"July 29. This morning, soon after breakfast, Sih, former Taoutai of Shanghai, now chief judge of Kiang-Soo, made his appearance at our abode. He came to the capital somewhat in advance of the Imperial commissioners, Kwei-liang and Hwa-sha-na. Doubtless he is regarded as a strong pillar of the anti-foreign party, and is here for the purpose of defeating the ends we have in view. Every interview in which he bears a part proves him to be the possessor both of sagacity and influence. His presence at court does not augur well for our success in negotiation. His object to-day was to arrange a meeting to-morrow between our minister and the Chinese commissioners. To our surprise he broached the subject of an interview with the Emperor, and the performance of the ceremony (three kneelings and nine prostrations) as the necessary condition of said interview.

"What his real motive in making this ridiculous proposition is, it is impossible to determine. Perhaps he thinks that Mr. Ward might without particular thought conform to the court-ceremonial, and thus flatter celestial pride. More likely he hopes to gain his point of breaking off all intercourse with us by proposing conditions which he is assured we cannot accept. However, to-morrow's interview may throw more light on the matter. It was agreed according to the special request of the Chinese ministers that only four persons should proceed to the contemplated meeting. These are to be Mr. Ward and his brother, Dr. Williams and Mr. Martin.

"The weather continues moderately warm, the thermometer not rising above 90°.

"July 30. At 10½ o'clock the four gentlemen named yesterday proceeded under the guidance of several officers to the place of meeting, which was near the north-west corner of the Imperial city, in an edifice called the Kia-hing-sz. They were received in magnificent style by Kwei, Hwa, and Sih, attended by a host of inferior mandarins, adorned with buttons indicating various grades. Business was discussed over a dinner which was sufficient for a hundred epicures, though only seven persons had places at the table. The principal topic was the interview with his Imperial majesty, and the ceremony of 'knocking heads.'

"It appears that Kwei was less conciliatory and urbane than at Shanghai. It was even intimated that the recent event at Ta-koo should prove a warning to any nation that dared to set itself in opposition to the middle kingdom. The gentlemen returned at three o'clock under a burning sun, from the effects of which they have suffered more or less all day. They rode on horseback.

"Our situation is becoming daily more irksome. Hitherto our own Chinese servants have been permitted to go out at their pleasure; now, however, all egress is forbidden. Only my teacher, Hoo, still rejoices in his liberty. An exception is made in his favor on the ground of his being a northerner, but chiefly through the influence of a petty officer at the gate, who is a native of the same province with himself.

"We are all wondering why the Russians have not come near us. It may be that they stand on a point of Eastern etiquette, which requires the last comer to pay the first visit. The more probable explanation is that the Chinese authorities will not permit them to follow their own inclination in the matter. And yet it seems strange that the Russians should allow themselves to be thus restricted.

"The principal fruits furnished to us thus far are apples, plums, pears, peaches, and water-melons. The last only can compare in flavor with home fruit.

"I succeeded in obtaining to-day through Hoo, three pieces of Peking bronze-work, not very handsome, but still valuable. One represents a stag on which a man is mounted. The other two are a pair of birds with long legs and necks, probably a species of crane. If on Monday we should be compelled to take our departure suddenly, I shall carry away some memorial of this visit.

"How strange that Saturday evening finds me in this mighty capital, beneath the shadow of a throne, whose occupant rules over one-third of the human race! It seems like a dream of the night.

"July 31. Sabbath. A calm, delicious, quiet day. So still have we been in our quarters that one could have imagined himself in a retired country village of New England. But alas! no church bells were heard calling the Lord's people to their solemn assemblies. We knew that all around us were the hum of business and the whirl of pleasure as on other days. God, however, received the homage of some sincere souls even here. At eleven o'clock we met in our dining-room, and united in prayer and praise to God, the Father, the Son, and the Holy Ghost. Rev. Mr. Wood, the chaplain, preached an appropriate sermon from the words, 'And hath broken down the middle wall of partition between us.' Eph. ii. 14. In the afternoon Mr. Ward, Dr. Williams, and myself spent two hours in reading aloud and conversing about the First Epistle of Timothy. This evening we had quite a number present at worship. Each night of our worship has added one or more to our praying circle. After the regular exercises we united in singing, 'Glory to Thee, my God, this night,' and 'From Greenland's icy mountains.' Oh! how vividly and sadly were things of the past brought to my recollection. Oh! that I could again hear in the sweet songs of Zion the dear voices which now echo only through the halls of memory! Truly in circumstances like these,

> 'I feel like one who treads alone
> Some banquet-hall deserted,
> Whose lights are fled, whose garlands dead,
> And all but he departed.'

"With what unutterable longings do I anticipate the joyful day when long-severed ties shall be reunited, and neither death nor distance shall be permitted to interrupt the hallowed intercourse of friendship! That day may yet be distant, and I therefore pray for grace to wait its coming patiently, and to fill the intervening space with works of piety and usefulness.

"August 1. Mr. Martin and myself received a

visit from the officers, the one with a blue, the other with a crystal ball. The former commands the guard at four of the city gates. They showed a fair amount of intelligence in conversation. What their precise object was could not be ascertained. Probably it was to get a look at our interior arrangements. We showed them various foreign articles, with which they seemed pleased.

"Aug. 2. Kwei, Hwa, and Sih returned the visit of Mr. Ward, and renewed the discussion which was commenced at the previous interview. They arrived at eleven o'clock in chariots, Kwei's being different from those in ordinary use in having the wheels quite at the hinder end. After a long and warm discussion, at which only our minister, Dr. Williams, Mr. Ward's brother, and Mr. Martin were present, all retired to our dining-room, where a sumptuous entertainment was prepared chiefly by themselves. Sih himself came here early in the morning to oversee the arrangement of the tables. At one table sat those who had been engaged in the discussion with the three Chinese commissioners, at the other all the officers of Mr. Ward's suite. Not feeling very well, I retired to my own room, and was glad to enjoy its quiet repose.

"The subject of the business part of the interview was the proposed audience with the Emperor. The only difficulty lay in the matter of the ceremony. At an early stage of the debate, the idea of asking our minister to perform it *in toto* was abandoned. The trouble was to ascertain what could be substituted for it by way of compromise. Mr. Ward took the ground that he would adhere to the custom followed by the United States ambassadors everywhere, *i. e.*, that he would meet the Emperor as he would the President of the United States, with a low bow, and repeat it if necessary. The Chinese were only anxious to have him promise to kneel on one knee, were it with ever so slight an inclination. They proposed to express the ceremony by the words, 'slightly bending on one knee,' but Mr. Ward wisely refused to give his consent to such phraseology. So the matter for the present ended. On Thursday the judge will come to announce the decision which may be reached.

"While the debate was going on inside, a few officers of considerably high rank were wandering about the courts and passages. Among these were two who wore red balls, indicating the high station they held. One of these was a youth of seventeen, the nephew of Hwa-sha-na. The other is a professor in the national college, who figured somewhat prominently last year at Tientsin, and who is known among us as the *Viscount.* I showed the former of these a few foreign articles, which I thought might interest him. His manners were exceedingly refined, and even winning. We were all much pleased with his behaviour. Should he live, he will doubtless rise to some of the highest offices in the Empire. My heart instinctively yearns to see such men brought under the power of the gospel. Alas! for their ignorance, and their consequent debasement!

"The Chinese seem determined to prevent all communication between us and the external world, except what is carried on through their minions, and under their supervision. The position we occupy is degrading to us, as subjects of a free and powerful kingdom.

"August 4. Sih, the judge, came according to promise, and after a discussion of more than three hours with Dr. Williams, announced the decision of his superiors to this effect: That Mr. Ward might have an interview with the Emperor, only performing the ceremony usual with foreigners when introduced to our President, or with our public functionaries when introduced to foreign princes. He made a desperate effort to gain the consent of Mr. Ward to bow so low that the ends of his fingers would touch the ground. But this also was flatly refused. The interview is to take place next Monday, the ratified treaties are to be exchanged on Tuesday; Wednesday, Thursday and Friday are to be devoted to sight-seeing, under the guidance of high officers; and on Saturday morning we set out on our return. Such is the pleasing programme as now arranged; but 'we know not what a day may bring forth.'

"This evening two or more Russians came to the door of our residence and demanded admittance. The petty officers at the door objected stoutly. Some of our people came in to inform us. Dr. Williams and myself went out to meet them, but they had already gone, and every Chinaman at the gate denied that any Russian had been near. Such downright lies they are guilty of whenever it suits their convenience. Although we have been more than a week here no visits have been exchanged with the Russians. So jealous are the authorities that they even kept back for several days a communication addressed to Mr. Ward, in answer to one of his forwarded immediately on our arrival.

"I should not forget to mention that the Chinese are fully aware of our violation of neutrality on the 25th of June. It has been distinctly spoken of in the last two interviews with the judge. Nor can all our protestations make them believe that some of our force was not joined with the English in the attempt to storm the batteries. Their willingness to continue the negotiations in spite of our error on that day, shows that for some reason, doubtless a selfish one, they are very unwilling to break with us at present."

CHAPTER XX.

His Sickness—Death—Character.

WITH the closing words of the last chapter the journal of the good man, whose chequered life we have tried faithfully to follow, abruptly terminates; and these were probably the last lines traced by his truthful hand. Manifestly he knew not what was before him. We have already seen that he had but little hope of effecting a settlement as a missionary in the capital, after that disastrous repulse of the French and English at the mouth of the Peiho. And yet it was something to pass through and survey the land; something to visit the greatest city in the world, the capital of the greatest and oldest empire of the globe; something, with fellow-missionaries, even temporarily to offer prayer and praise to the one only living and true God in that stronghold of hoary superstitions and degrading idolatry, and he held on his way.

That journey, however, from the coast in midsummer, was not calculated to recruit the wasted energies of a partial invalid, especially the last part, over that rough, broken pavement, in a springless, jolting cart, fantastically called "chariot." In a letter from the capital, dated Aug. 3d, one day before the last entry in the journal, Mr. Aitchison complained more than was his wont of the fatigues and discomforts of this trip, and spoke of the grateful shades under which he sat many times to rest during the latter part of the way. One who knew him well could have seen that he was already sick, as rest was what he seldom sought in other days. Work here, rest in heaven, was all he thought of while in health.

Mr. Aitchison was sadly disappointed in the results of this expedition, so far as this world was concerned; not so, we are persuaded, of the next. Although our Minister and suite were ostentatiously conducted, amidst thronging crowds of curious spectators, to the quarters prepared for them, and there attended with almost an endless retinue of servants and officials, every want being perfectly supplied, yet they were strictly guarded and carefully confined to the rooms assigned them.

"From the moment we passed the threshold of our present abode to the present time, just one week," said Mr. Aitchison in the letter of the 3d of August, to which allusion has been already made, "we have not been permitted to put our foot outside the door, and even our Chinese servants are prohibited from going out. This is nothing more than what my previous acquaintance with Chinese history and notions led me to expect, but notwithstanding it is very provoking. To remain a week within the walls of a city abounding in objects of surpassing interest, without being permitted to gaze upon one, is tantalizing to the last degree. I need not go into a very particular explanation of the causes which lead to such treatment. Such is, and has been from time immemorial, the *policy* of China. She fears everything external to herself. We are in fact, though not in name, *prisoners*."

But God was at the door ready to knock off the chains of one of those prisoners, and set him free to range at will, through a larger city and a greater capital, even, than that of "the Central,

Celestial, Flowery Kingdom." The very next day Mr. Aitchison was taken sick; and yet he thought not seriously so, and no physician was called for three or four days. His disease (dysentery) was not then alarming; but Mr. Aitchison himself felt that the time of his deliverance had come. "His nervous system," as Mr. Williams expressed it, "sank more rapidly than his muscular." Those who knew him best will somewhat understand this. For five years earth had contained few attractions for him, heaven many. His private letters made frequent mention of his longings after heaven. Not that he was unwilling to work just so long as the Master required; but when, consistently with all the interests of his glorious kingdom, he seemed to be often saying, the release might come, the sooner the better. He had often expressed the conviction, especially after the death of his colleague, Mr. Macy, that his life would not be long, and had spoken joyfully with some of his dearest friends of the blessed change for which he hoped. In such a state of mind he gave specific directions on leaving Shanghai on this last expedition, with regard to his effects, in case he should not return—so was his lamp always trimmed and burning.

On the 11th of August, after he had been sick a week, the embassy left the capital to return to the coast. It was with great reluctance that they attempted to remove the patient in his feeble condition, and yet it was judged best, all things considered, the physician giving it as his opinion that his chances for recovery would be greatly enhanced if he should survive to reach the sea. The first twelve miles of the journey was again over that wretched, broken pavement; but Mr. Aitchison could not now resort to the alternative of walking for relief. They carried the poor, patient sufferer in a litter, or palanquin, somewhat peculiar in construction, and borne, not by men, but by two mules, harnessed into the opposite ends of two long poles, as into thills, one preceding and one following the occupant. This was perhaps as comfortable a conveyance as could have been devised for the purpose; but the sufferings of the sick man were very great, both before, and at the time of his removal.

After reaching Tung-Chow in this way, they were three days and four nights in their boats descending the river. During all this time every attention and kindness possible in the circumstances were bestowed upon the poor sufferer. Dr. Fox, the surgeon of the Powhatan and the attending physician in the case, was unwearied in his efforts for his recovery. Rev. Mr. Martin watched over him by day and by night as a faithful nurse and friend, and afterward gave in the North China Herald a minute account of these last days, to which we are indebted for these interesting particulars. Other members also of the expedition did what they could; but all in vain. His disease was indeed soon subdued, but the recuperative powers of the system were gone, and he was rapidly sinking to his final rest. As strength failed reason became unsettled; he talked incoherently, but even then, Mr. Martin says, "All his aspirations were heavenward, his thoughts love, and his broken ejaculations yearnings after a higher and holier life." He often expressed also his desire to be released from the body. "Now lettest thou thy servant depart in peace," was frequently on his fevered lips. "Let me go—why will you detain me?" was his gentle remonstrance with the kind friends around him.

In a more lucid interval, however, the night before his death, he gave clear expression to his unwavering faith in Christ. "I have served my Master," he said, "with great imperfection, but my trust is in his atoning blood. And on this expedition, I have been betrayed into some inconsistencies"—mark the honesty of this confession—"but still I have enjoyed hours of sweet communion with God." So far he had spoken quietly on this occasion; then rising with a convulsive spring, and gazing up into heaven, as if absorbed with visions of ecstatic glory, he exclaimed, "I see Jesus, and all the prophets!" and "pouring out his soul in sublime strains of prayer and praise," Mr. Martin tells us, "he closed with the doxology, 'Hosanna! hosanna in the highest!'"

This was Sabbath evening—the last he spent on earth. He was on a Chinese boat, on a Chinese river, sixteen thousand miles away from nearly all his dearest relatives and friends on earth. What a comfort in those hours of pain and anguish to have had a mother or sister bending over his troubled couch, wiping the death-damps from his brow. But for love of souls he had left all these, and God was with him. He remembered several absent friends; sent thanks to some for their kindness to him in other days, and messages of affection to others. He made special mention of Mr. Burdon, the bosom friend and companion of so large a part of his missionary life. "Tell him," said he to Mr. Martin, starting from an uneasy slumber, "that I loved him tenderly and devotedly, and I loved him to the last. We shall not be long separated; then we shall be with our wives in heaven. Tell him to be faithful unto death; and I say the same to you, and to all my Shanghai friends."

At a late hour, a Chinese prefect, *Le* by name, came to see him; and taking him by the hand, informed him that to avoid the heat of the day, he was appointed to escort him on his journey early the next morning in advance of the rest of the company. "*Wo-taow-t'ang-kien, yung-yuen-yei-fuh*"—"I am going to heaven, to everlasting blessedness," was the emphatic reply, which may cleave to the memory of that mandarin to his dying day, and perhaps lead him also to the blessedness anticipated by the dying Christian.

"That young Hebrew—through what difficulties he has had to struggle," was an exclamation which burst from a mass of inarticulate sounds, and indicated that the object of so much of his solicitude and faithful labors on board the Powhatan, still shared his dying thoughts.

When some of his fellow-travellers came to inquire for his welfare, he exhorted them tenderly and earnestly to make their calling and election sure. When Dr. Williams and Mr. Martin were together by his bedside, he requested them to repeat to him the exceeding great and precious promises, and to sing him some of the songs of Zion. He attempted to join with his feeble faltering voice. After singing a while they read to him several of his favorite hymns, pausing for him to repeat such passages as he was still able to recollect.

Thus wore away the Sabbath night. Early on Monday morning, the 15th of August, the embassy left the river, and started again by land. There remained thirty-five hours of this part of the journey before reaching the ships. Gently they lifted the sufferer again into his palanquin, and gently they started on their way. Dr. Fox was incessant in his attentions and kindness, coming often to the litter to see how the patient was, or to administer some cordial for his comfort. About five hours of the weary way were thus passed, while it was evident that the sick one was rapidly losing what little strength remained in the morning, and that the hope of his reaching the sea was fast ebbing forever away. About eleven o'clock in the forenoon, the doctor came once more to look upon his patient, gave some stimulant to help sustain if possible a little longer the failing energies, and then left him. Coming again after a few moments—a very few—he found that the weary spirit had already taken its flight; and William Aitchison, the true Christian, the ripe scholar, the loving friend, the devoted missionary had closed his eyes in death, all unseen and unattended, except as the angels came to bear him in triumph to the bosom of his God and Saviour.

This event occurred near the town of Pehtang, not far from the banks of the Peiho, and about thirty hours' journey from the sea, where the ships of the Embassy were then lying. His age was thirty-three years and seven months. His remains were carried to Pehtang, where they arrived the next afternoon. A strong Chinese coffin was procured, with the intention of taking them back to Shanghai, to bury him by the side of his beloved colleague, Mr. Macy, which would have been a great gratification to the missionaries there. But this the weather did not permit. Thirty hours had already elapsed since his death; decomposition had commenced, and they were compelled to commit his body to the deep.

This was done on the evening of the 18th, with every demonstration of affection and respect. After running out into ten fathoms of water, the two steamers lay to, hoisted their colors at half-mast, and then was heard the solemn cry: "Ho, all hands, bury the dead." The Minister and Commodore, with many officers of their respective suites, passed to the deck of the Taiwan, where the burial service was devoutly read by the chaplain of the frigate, and then the coffin, with its precious freight, was reverently passed over the side of the ship and lowered into the unfolding waves of the Gulf of Pichili, a part of the China Sea, there to rest until the sea shall give up its dead.

Singular, and almost prophetic, were some

lines of a little poem written by Mr. Aitchison twelve years before, and published in the Yale Literary Magazine in 1847, entitled "The Time to die." It consists of five stanzas. We transcribe only the last two.

"Bury me not at the close of day,
When the twilight softly fades away,
When a deathlike stillness fills the air,
And goodness kneels at the place of prayer.
Be not the church-yard my place of rest,
Let no hallowed dust fall on my breast,
Where sleep my fathers, let me not sleep,
May loved ones over my grave ne'er weep.

"But let me die at the midnight hour,
When winds howl loud, and dark clouds low'r;
With no friend near to close my fixed eye,
Or bend his ear for my last faint sigh.
Let no speaking marble mark the spot,
Where 'neath the clods my body shall rot;
There let me rest from earth's toilsome strife,
Till God shall wake me to endless life."

Not beneath the clods of the valley, as we have seen, but beneath the waves of the sea, his body sleeps and waits the resurrection morn; and so his lonely wanderings ceased, and his happy spirit ascended to the loved ones gone before, to that blessed Saviour who had stood by him and strengthened him amid all the trials of his pilgrimage.

He leaves, of his own immediate relatives, father, mother, and two sisters, to mourn his loss,—but not long. Many friends, beside wife, child, and father-in-law, have already joined "the innumerable caravan;" many since he left these shores; and, singularly, also, not long after his decease, that beautiful, embowered dwelling, in which he once thought to find all the blessedness contained in that matchless word *home*, took fire and burned to the ground. So is Providence saying to all who read: "This is not your rest."

But will any one think that his life was thrown away? It was given to God, to whom we all belong; it was devoted to the noblest cause which can engage the energies of the human soul; it was adorned with the highest and purest virtues; and neither man nor angel can yet tell how much good it has already accomplished by its sweet and hallowed influence on all within its reach, or how much more it may effect in many generations to come. Although he fell in his youthful prime, his name still lives, and he will long be remembered as one of the early, earnest, useful missionaries of the cross in China. And although he could not himself settle down and labor in the capital of that vast kingdom, he is the forerunner of those who will. His name will yet be mentioned there; and devout lips of happy worshipers of his God and Saviour will yet tell their fellow-countrymen, how a good man once came from the far off lands of the setting sun, and tried to bear the message of salvation through a crucified Redeemer, even to the gates of the Imperial palace; and as the converts of other generations sail over the gulf of Pichili, they will drop a tear to the memory of the young missionary who once had great thoughts and great plans for China's welfare, but was compelled to leave them all to other heads and other hands, as his weary mortal frame sank to its long rest beneath those unquiet waves.

So the good man ceased from his labors. Many mourned as for a standard-bearer fallen; and many were the letters of sympathy and condolence received by his friends, showing the high appreciation of his character cherished by others.

The senior Secretary of the American Board

Five Years in China.

The Cemetery at Shanghai, China.

P. 277.

speaks of "his talents, his scholarship, his piety, and his enlarged benevolence, his devotion to the spiritual renovation of a great and benighted people, and his eminently consistent and beautiful life," and calls him "one of the most devoted and promising missionaries ever in China."

The fellow-missionaries of Mr. Aitchison, of all denominations, deeply felt his loss. The Rev. Mr. Burdon, his associate and friend in so large a part of his missionary life, was called upon to preach a funeral sermon in the chapel of the London Missionary Society, where Mr. Aitchison had often officiated with great acceptance. He took for his text the dying message of the young soldier of the cross: "Be thou faithful unto death."

To the memory of Mr. Aitchison a fitting monument was raised by the missionaries in their little cemetery at Shanghai, telling the story of his early death. Here the beloved and lamented Macy was buried, and over his grave a marble shaft had been erected by his Chinese friends, a voluntary tribute of admiration and love to one who had laid down his life for their nation. Beside this pillar, and like it in shape, was the monument raised to the memory of Aitchison. United in life, in death they were not long divided. The Rev. Elijah C. Bridgman, who, in the illustration, leans upon the grave-stone, with the fall of the autumn leaves was laid beside the horizontal slab near which he stands.*

The Rev. Mr. Blodget, his associate in studies and labors most of the time for fifteen years, thus speaks of his attainments and worth:—In the short space of five years he had learned to speak with fluency, distinctness, and accuracy both the Shanghai and the court dialect. He wrote the Chinese characters with an ease and elegance such as I have not seen equaled by any foreigner. He had read extensively in the Chinese classics. Yet he regarded himself but as a beginner, and accounted that ten years at least would be necessary before he should be fully competent to literary labor. Two short works, one on the geography of the Scriptures, and another giving a summary of their books and their contents had been prepared by him, and will be published."

The Rev. Mr. Martin, his associate and com-

* For this illustration we are indebted to the authoress of the Life of Dr. Bridgman.

panion on his last trip, speaks of him as "one whose talents and virtues commanded the respect of all who knew him; and who, though comparatively recent in his arrival in China, was already far advanced in the way to eminence as a Chinese scholar and a missionary."

And Rev. Mr. Cunnyngham, another missionary, wrote:—"To know him was to respect, to love him. He was among his companions here a universal favorite. As a preacher he stood very high among his brethren. As a Chinese scholar, taking the length of time he had been in the field, he had not his equal among us. To this, not only the missionaries bear cheerful testimony, but the Chinese scholars invariably so regarded him. We had come to look upon him as the most promising young man among the American missionaries."

Such was the candid estimate of wise and competent men in regard to the character and labors of Mr. Aitchison. The prime elements of his power and usefulness are so clearly manifest in all the record of his daily life, that further attempts to elucidate them would seem superfluous; his sweet simplicity, his genuine good sense, his native politeness, his true benevolence, and above all, his devoted, constant piety—these, with God's blessing, lifted him from his humble sphere in the Norwich cotton mill, and set him among men of influence and renown; these made him the true friend, the prudent counsellor, the judicious and indefatigable worker, useful and beloved in every position which he was called to fill. Born in Scotland, educated in America, laboring and dying in China, he belonged to no one land alone, but to all the world, to God, and to heaven.

APPENDIX.

The following obituary notice of Mrs. Aitchison appeared at the time of her death in one of the leading religious journals of New York:—

"From her earliest youth she gave promise of uncommon excellence. She possessed superior native powers, enriched by judicious culture; an imagination which clothed everything in beauty to her eyes; a taste refined and exquisite; a buoyant disposition, hopeful even to the latest hour of life, and a heart warm, constant, and confiding.

"She was a lover of the beautiful in whatever form it existed. Especially did she delight in the works of nature, often expressing the opinion that a person became a better and a holier Christian by communion with God in his works. Her enthusiasm in regard to trees and flowers and birds was remarkable. Music and poetry were the natural outgushings of such a heart, gladdening her own life, and delighting all who were privileged with her friendship. She had not many intimate friends. To a chosen few in whom she could confide, she opened her heart freely, and they found in it a wealth of affection of which others could form no idea. Perhaps no one looked forward into life with brighter hopes.

"But it was as a Christian that her chief loveliness was made manifest. She became a professed follower of the Saviour at the age of sixteen, and thenceforth her religious character was decided, consistent, humble, and cheerful. The writer was associated with her in a Mission Sabbath School in New Haven, for the space of four years, and can testify to the faithful discharge of her duties there, and her unwearied labors for the salvation of her scholars. The same which thus adorned her daily life, was her strength and support as she drew near the valley of the shadow of death. It was not a dark valley to her. For a year past, and particularly for the last eight or nine weeks of her life, she seemed to view death as before her; but there was nothing like gloom or despondency in her feelings for a moment. 'I am *happy*,' seemed to be the true expression of her life, as well as of her lips, in these last days. When the Master's call came suddenly at the last, in the middle of the night-watch, she was calm and tranquil. She had previously, in a perfectly clear and distinct voice, bidden each member of the family a separate 'good-bye;' and as the hours passed slowly on, she sat silently looking into the grave, and waiting for her change to come. The indescribable bodily distress of the three previous days had exhausted her strength, and now too faint to speak except by an occasional answer to a question from her husband, in one of which she said her only hope was in Christ, she was absorbed in quiet, trustful thought until the power of consciousness ceased. Fainter and fainter grew the pulsation of her heart, until at a quarter past 4 o'clock, on Wednesday morning, January 12th, it stood still forever."

The following lines were found in her portfolio after her decease, evidently the fruit of some prophetic musings, as the day of her departure seemed to be drawing near.

THE DEATH ROOM.

"Weary and spent and gasping low,
A young girl lay on a couch of snow,
With dim and death-closed eye;
Her form was wasted, wan and weak,
No bloom was left on her faded cheek—
The faintest word she could not speak—
This was her hour to die.

"Gently she bowed to the grim old king—
So fair and lovely and frail a thing
Could not resist him long.
She died—and loved ones standing by,
As her spirit flew to the upper sky,
Heard an angel voice in warble high,
Singing this happy song:—

"I have done with earth—I have done with pain,
And I am forever free;
I have broken away from my galling chain—
Redeemer, I come to Thee.

"I have bidden farewell to my earthly house,
So often racked with sorrow;
I feel no dread of the future now,
For eternity has no morrow.

"Dear friends, farewell! I shall love you still
Weep not o'er my ice-cold clay—
For a harp of gold, and a crown of life,
Are given to me to-day.

"Farewell!—Mourn not o'er the lifeless dust,
But lay it beneath the sod;
A glorious, happy spirit now,
I speed to the throne of God."

THE END.

www.ingramcontent.com/pod-product-compliance
Lightning Source LLC
LaVergne TN
LVHW020238110826
845151LV00003B/955

* 9 7 8 1 4 2 5 5 2 9 4 2 0 *